THE GOLDEN THREAD

THE GOLDEN THREAD
A MEMOIR

K. CATES

Copyright © 2007, 2014 K. Cates.

Edited by Dionne Jones and Alice Peck.

All rights reserved. No part of this book may be used or reproduced by any means, graphic, electronic, or mechanical, including photocopying, recording, taping or by any information storage retrieval system without the written permission of the publisher except in the case of brief quotations embodied in critical articles and reviews.

Archway Publishing books may be ordered through booksellers or by contacting:

Archway Publishing
1663 Liberty Drive
Bloomington, IN 47403
www.archwaypublishing.com
1-(888)-242-5904

Because of the dynamic nature of the Internet, any web addresses or links contained in this book may have changed since publication and may no longer be valid. The views expressed in this work are solely those of the author and do not necessarily reflect the views of the publisher, and the publisher hereby disclaims any responsibility for them.

Any people depicted in stock imagery provided by Thinkstock are models, and such images are being used for illustrative purposes only. Certain stock imagery © Thinkstock.

ISBN: 978-1-4808-1146-1 (sc)
ISBN: 978-1-4808-1154-6 (hc)
ISBN: 978-1-4808-1147-8 (e)

Library of Congress Control Number: 2014917010

Printed in the United States of America.

Archway Publishing rev. date: 10/13/2014

AUTHOR'S NOTE

This book is dedicated to family and friends, who are still willing or able to call me a friend, in spite of myself. Thank you to the neighborhood, our church, to all those who loved us, you are etched into our hearts. Thanks to my parents, you're why I became anything at all. My daughter, I would not be brave or sane, without you, thank you for the grace you grant your less than perfect parents. You are relentlessly loved by both of us. To my editors, Dionne Jones and Alice Peck you make sense of me for everyone else. Thank you Alicia and all the Simon&Schuster/Archway staff. To my son, for giving me unique perspective on my purpose.

All of us have threads. Various tiny, almost unnoticed lint flecks of life. Together they form a "fabric," an inner voice. A willy-nilly happening that seems not so "willy-nilly" after all. A sign that provides direction. Hope, at an insurmountable impasse.

As if by divine appointment, these threads direct us in life's chaos, though we can't always detect it. Millions of threads in a lifetime—frayed, sun bleached, and worn, as we grow old. They weave a tapestry that makes our lives. The fabric may even have holes, right from the factory. Woven around and through a golden thread, they can speak to us. About purpose. About ourselves. About God.

I am telling this story to the best of my ability, as accurately as memory serves. This is not a book of blame. I am not proud of all of my own choices. The names of the people in this book have been changed to protect their privacy. I removed my use of cuss words to prevent offense. It is my hope that through authenticity, this book will open dialogue that might not otherwise occur. Few are willing to talk as candidly as I for fear of shame. But I can look you in the eye, because this is a book about grace, love, and purpose.

Are you facing the greatest challenge of your life? Don't quit. *You are too close.*

CONTENTS

1   A Perfect Plan 1
2   Significance in the Little Things 11
3   Thirty Seconds Can Change Your Life 21
4   Good-Bye 29
5   Obsessions 39
6   Why? 49
7   Happy Holidays 61
8   Resurrection Sunday 69
9   The Pecan Pie Storm 77
10   Pinkie Swear 85
11   Bliss and Vinegar 89
12   More than Just Cheeseburgers in Paradise 99
13   The Breakdown 107
14   I'm Fine 121
15   Dirty Hands 133
16   Courage 145
17   The Twin 159
18   The Grave 171
19   Monarch Butterflies 175
20   Nothing, Nothing, Nothing Is Impossible, So Believe 189
21   What's the Answer? 201

CHAPTER 1

A Perfect Plan

I watched him in shock, as if outside of myself. Chad stood like a statue. Sunken shoulders. Rippling pain spread across his face. Stiff arms. A tendon in his jaw pulsed in distress. We were poised on either side of the bed in the kind of silence that only death can deliver. We tried not to speak or cry, but the dam broke. He hung like a caged gorilla, swaying as he held onto the bed rails. I had never imagined this. The weight of his anger rushed through the room like a tornado. He stopped to cradle lifelessness in his arms, as if afraid to remember the painful magnitude of what it represents in life, while in fear of forgetting one miniscule detail or memory. I, the murderer, came here to say good-bye. Immediately, I realized I had killed not just one love, but two. Overwhelmed. Yes. I had come to say good-bye. But I had not prepared for Chad's emotional devastation, which transfixed me.

We held ourselves up, one on each side of the bed. Our knees buckled, slipping to the floor in ceaseless sobs, hanging from those railings. Seeing Chad at eye level under the raised surgical bed was like living beneath the life we had known, buried and suffocating in grief. We couldn't handle it.

We were an ordinary couple. Church once a month. Drinks with friends on the weekends. We had a moral compass. Happily married. Very much in love. A swear word here or there and a little "keeping up with the Joneses" in the early years but a good, normal life.

I married at twenty-five. My prince was the charming, very handsome boy next door, literally. With dark hair and eyes, Chad tanned like a Coppertone commercial and was any woman's dream in a suit and tie or unshaven and sweaty. Scuba diver's watch. Golf clubs in the trunk. Sales awards on the walls of his office. Driven, successful, and extremely well received, he won the hearts of many, personally and professionally. But he failed to see himself as one of the biggest winners in the game of life. Chad, whose name means "battle warrior," far exceeded my expectations of the man I would marry, and with him, I had everything I wanted on my journey to happiness. After three years, his singular weakness was his work addiction, which I accepted because it was his only flaw, and my attempts to undo it were futile.

I had found a good man, and I was blessed to join his family. Always warm, with outbursts of laughter and enjoyable dinner table conversations (if he wasn't working). The holidays at his parents' home were filled with spinach balls, linen-covered tables, crystal and silver serving dishes, and gourmet candlelight dinners, while peaceful music serenaded beneath the laughter. Chad's mother could make an occasion out of any event. We often played a game called Five Hundred Rummy, which built camaraderie and gave us reasons to share stories and eat more pecan pie. They reflected my strengths and weaknesses in contrast to my own experiences. And they loved me, in spite of my blunt opinions and long-winded chatter.

My parents were similar, in that we shared faith, the "ceremony" of any event, and the sacredness of the blood-related institution. My uncle was a Pentecostal minister, while Chad had a third cousin who was a priest.

Three years after our wedding, we went to a doctor's office to determine whether there would be any conception challenges, and we learned it might be difficult to conceive. Surprised and disappointed, we didn't speak of it all day.

That night, under the covers, we started talking.

"We can try. If it doesn't work, we have options." I smiled.

I asked Chad if he would be willing to put his hand on my stomach and pray with me.

"I think God is punishing me, because I've made some mistakes in my past." He grunted.

"Aw, honey, God doesn't punish us. That's why, when we believe and pray for forgiveness, He is a loving God. Mercy and forgiveness. That's the whole point of Christ."

"I don't believe that God is *that* involved in the details. He gave us life. We make the most of it. You know I don't believe in prayer."

"Sometimes, that's all we have. Sometimes God doesn't change the circumstance, although He can, and sometimes He changes *us*." I smiled, knowing from his heaving sigh that I had said enough.

"What is the downside, Chad? We get a perfect baby?"

He reluctantly agreed. I placed his hand on my tummy and mine on his and uttered a simple request for a boy, per Chad's preference. Little did we know that the seed planted that day would lead us to the most character-building event of both of our lives.

I learned I was pregnant two weeks later, and calculations proved that I had already been pregnant when we prayed. Before we asked, it had already been answered. How many times in my life have those small, immaterial occurrences come to have the highest value?

Nine months later, a healthy, white-haired baby boy was born. We named him Malak, which means messenger.

A year and a half after Malak's birth, we had a perfect, blonde baby girl named Grace, which means blessing or favor. She grew to be the queen of our house, adding ribbons and bows everywhere, which only enhanced Malak's big-brother testosterone.

From the beginning, Chad and I felt that moral thoughtfulness was a trait necessary to raising our kids, so when they were old enough to understand, we came up with a family creed. A motto to live by. After a meeting, the four- and five-year-old hung it on the refrigerator. The goal was to recite it in the mornings until we understood and absorbed the principles. It still hangs in my house today:

> The Family Creed
> *I am a gift from God.*
> *I am thankful.*
> *I am loved.*
> *I am special.*
> *I am intelligent.*
> *I am honest.*
> *I am peaceful.*
> *I am kind.*
> *I am a good listener.*
> *I will be kind to others and myself.*
> *I will pray.*
> *I will follow Jesus with my head, my hands, and my heart.*
> *Every day is a happy day.*

And every day *was* a happy day. I had my perfect tapestry, made in the design I had always dreamed of. Woven by me, for me. The perfect cover, the perfect warmth, a glorious decoration. I had everything I ever wanted, and I thanked God for it.

But the joyful days wouldn't last.

Four years later, at six o'clock on a Thursday morning in November, in our second-story bedroom in South Chicago, Chad woke me.

"I just heard the front door close. Did you lock the door last night?"

"Yeah."

"Are you sure?" he asked, confused.

"Yeah."

"Stay here. I'll go downstairs."

Off he went, my dragon-slayer. Chivalry was not dead. Sometimes his left ear's hearing wasn't good, maybe from the noise of a gun when he was hunting as a boy. Maybe he had imagined the sound. He was my hero, my king, and my confidant, and his arm muscles never looked better. What woman doesn't want a hero at a time like this? When he got downstairs, he called to me, laughing, "Come here! You *gotta* see *this*!"

At the front door, I found my little man, five-year-old Malak, barefoot, race-car-pajama-clad, with hockey stick poised at the puck in the frozen, snow-dusted yard. I shivered, thinking his feet must be numb, but he loved hockey enough to endure the cold! Twenty degrees on the front step, I entered the kitchen to warm up. On the floor was one bag of opened hot dogs, two of which were MIA. The juice trail led me to the garage, where I found one twelve-inch butcher knife, resting on the garage step, removed from its proper placement in the butcher block atop the refrigerator. A long trail of hot dog juice escorted me to the remains of an additional empty hot dog bag on the table. Whoa. He could have hurt himself climbing up there, the fearless one!

We moved a year later, the summer before Malak went to kindergarten, to a small apartment with a pool, as our dream house was under construction. We spent captivating days at the pool, eating goldfish crackers and cheese, pretzels, and pop. The best part for me was when Malak and Grace snuggled next to Mommy with the shivers. Midwesterners gasp for a breath of fresh air and for the healing infusion of the sun and laughter that seems to elevate the level of our happiness, if for three short months, and then evaporate into memory. School would soon start.

One night, I went to tuck Malak into bed in that apartment. I bent down and kissed his tan cheek, blew a "zerbert" on his tummy with giggles, and played with his white-blond bowl-cut hair. It seemed to dance on his head. When I went to kiss him one last time, Malak squirmed and fidgeted as I pulled the sheets up under his chin. He looked as though his skin was crawling, and in a fearful outburst Malak shouted, "Mom, I saw a demon in my room!"

I never allowed television other than PBS or children's videos of puppies, rabbits, or Kermit the Frog. I was blindsided. How would he even know what a demon was? Where would he see one? I couldn't fathom. My maternal and religious instincts kicked in.

"Where is it, Malak?"

"It ran over there." He pointed to the corner of the room.

I saw nothing. *Could it have been a mouse?* "What did it look like, baby?"

"It had big scary teeth, huge pointy ears, and an ugly long tail. I don't wanna look, Mommy!"

Now I was in mental overdrive. Confused and afraid, I prayed, "In the name of Jesus, I curse anything evil in this room or in this apartment. I bind you, Devil, from anything harmful. I cast out demons and anything filthy from this room. This is holy ground. This is a holy house. We are a holy family. Thank You, Lord, for Your hedge of protection. Malak is hidden in the shadow of the almighty God, protected from anything evil. I give angels charge over us to keep us safe. Thank you, Jesus."

As I said these words, I heard the strangest sound outside of his open window, unlike anything I'd heard before in my life. It was the sound of a wild animal screaming but not a typical house cat or cougar. I find it hard to describe. It was forceful, like a lion, but angry and shrill. I closed the window and finished praying. This was the first of many times that I realized my son's uncommon awareness of a spiritual world that I did not know.

Smitten by his little dimpled smile and trying to cover my own fears, I said, "I love you like a peanut butter and jelly sandwich on a rainy day. Night-night, baby Malak."

"I love you more than the biggest thunderstorm, Mommy. I love you more than the drops of water in anywhere. I love you faster than a cheetah. I love you so much, my heart hurts, Mommy."

How did a little mind perceive and so carve out his words better than

I had, with all my years of trying? I guess this was my first experience with anything supernatural. I had heard stories. Since I didn't see the demon myself (thankfully), I pondered the mystery of a child who could describe one. It bothered me. Enough, to ignore it. Why had this demon visited my son, if it *was* true? We were a praying family. What did it mean? Had it come to warn us? This was, the first fleck of lint—a hint, giving me sign, I suppose. It was a loose thread that could unravel the whole garment of my life. A tear in the fabric often starts with a small snag.

Malak's first day of kindergarten was harried. I called out repeatedly for him while hustling to put the last touch-ups on my mascara and slipping on my white Keds. I refilled the vase of fuchsia roses from Chad. Gracie was right on my heels. But no Malak. Minutes passed. I panicked.

"Malak! Where are you? This isn't funny!"

Suddenly, I heard a quiet, muffled voice from the front closet. "Here I am. I'm in here," he said with an obedient but resigned tone. I opened the door and found Malak squished behind the vacuum cleaner. He crawled out.

"Sweetheart, what are you doing in there?"

"I'm scared," he said.

"Scared? Honey, what are you scared of?"

"My first day at the new school, Mommy. I don't wanna go."

"Aw, okay, baby. Tell you what; I promise that I won't leave you until you feel better. Is that a deal?"

"Deal," he whimpered. He reached for my hand, giving me a lower-lip pout.

Once at school, still holding his hand tightly in my grasp, we peered into the small classroom window. A wonderful prize of a little girl, Rachel, from our new neighborhood, took Malak's hand and gently walked him to the circle on the floor. They sat down, and she scooched closer to him and put her arm around him, patting him gently. I smiled as I watched. This would be a day to remember. Forever.

"Gracie, should we go to the grocery store?" I scooped her up, placing her on my hip with a kiss on her cheek.

"Mama, can we get some canny?"

"Sure. Candy it is." She gave me a butterfly kiss.

I never thought about the significance of these days or many other seemingly minor details … that are *not* minor details at all. We were living the ordinary/extraordinary that most of us miss. Though the little ones in our lives can be exhausting, they are jewels. Darlings. The biggest gift. Not little monsters, little fockers, or demons, as one might describe them. These are precious seconds. Beautiful hours. Minutes that turn into years that we can forget easily—the value of the kisses; the friendships that make life less scary; love that breathes something magical into an otherwise chore-driven to-do list every single day of our lives. These are the promises of something good in the world. Love is the promise of something good in the world.

Believe in yourself more often. Not more often. All the time. "As a man thinketh in his heart, so is he." —Proverbs 23:7

— CHAPTER 2 —

Significance in the Little Things

Everything in life was particularly perfect. Why did I feel ... uneasy? Couples frequently disagree on religion or faith. We were no different. We never missed church when we dated. We rarely missed church when we were married. Chad held my hand many Sundays in the pew. I told Chad the demon story the moment he got home. It bothered him; I could tell by the far-off look on his face, as if he were explaining it in his mind. The rest of the night, he looked thoughtful and somber, but we didn't discuss it.

In spite of our differences on prayer, we were very compatible. We golfed together and liked to travel. We were conservative on politics, financial matters, and child raising. I felt we were happier and stronger than most couples. I didn't care for hunting—most women don't (so shoot me). We did enjoy a juicy filet mignon or a chance to go deep-sea fishing.

One Saturday afternoon after working in the yard, I was interrupted. "Hey, beautiful!" Chad surprised me with a pinch on the butt and a kiss from behind.

"Hi! Are you looking for trouble, mister? I'm armed with the tree trimmer and dangerous, boy." I laughed.

I had a silly idea. I was not often as playful as I'd have liked. As task-driven as we were, even if unfortunately, our to-do lists rarely overlapped. I called the kids into the kitchen. In a firm voice but with a big toothy grin, I said, "Malak, lay down on the kitchen floor. Grace, lay down right next to him."

"Why, Mama?" Gracie asked.

"Just do it. You're gonna like this," I said, half sergeant, half silly. I snickered all the way to the drawer. Got two big spoons. Grabbed a secret from the cupboard. "Piper, come here, girl!" I yelled out the back door, and in came the family black lab, licking her slobbery gums. "Piper, sit. Sit. Stay. Be nice ... Okay. Kids, pull up your shirts and hold them up."

They started wriggling and squirming nervously on the wood floor. I took the spoons with peanut butter on them from behind my back and spread the peanut butter on their bellies. Piper got to lap up the peanut butter. Oh, we split our sides, wiping tears through laughter, while the kids could barely catch their breath from the relentless tickles.

"Okay, Piper. That's enough," Chad said, sighing with relief.

Chad grabbed me around the waist and gave me those puppy eyes. I loved the puppy eyes. In his famous Donald Duck impression, he said, "Awwwww ... I love you, pretty girl." That was what won me over on our first date. He would laugh with some embarrassment, but I melted every single time. Lucky girl. Charmed life.

Every once in a while, I added another journal page to the memory book I had started for the kids. I was neglectful in documenting their childhood memories. Five short entries had been written. Compelled to record another one, when my pen hit the paper, this entry focused on the man who had graced me with two children and life's limitless meaning.

> *Dear Malak and Gracie,*
>
> *I want you to know how much I love your father. He is so intelligent, so well liked by everybody, so good at any job he ever had. He is a humble man, a great friend, and a very loyal husband and daddy. He loves you so much. He never comes home late without checking on you while you lie sleeping in your beds. He gives each of you kisses. Sometimes, he sits and watches you.*
>
> *He's an honest man, sometimes to a fault. Occasionally when he makes a mistake, he will be good about admitting it. Your daddy would cross any ocean and climb any mountain to reach you. He is my best friend, and I love him more every day—not because I have to, but because it's a privilege to. He is always so proud of you, as am I.*
>
> *Love always,*
> *Mom*

That was the last entry in that journal. Over the years, Chad worked tirelessly in finance to provide us with a great life, and he delivered beyond any wife's expectation. I loved being married to him, cherished his family, and all that was woven in a fine garment more magnificent than I could have sewn on my own. Balancing his drive with his distaste for being anything mediocre often cost him his time with us, like many young men with the boldness and determination to excel in their career choices.

Often, I dialed his number on any given working day. Small talk at first but ending with the same question for him: "I love you, honey. Thank you for the gorgeous roses you brought home again last night. How are you today?"

"Oh, good. I'm working late. I have a dinner with clients, so I won't be home for dinner," he grumbled.

"So what time will you be home so I can kiss your face?"

"Late. I don't know."

"Like ten o'clock, or …"

"I don't … I gotta get back to it. I love you, dear. I'm glad you liked the flowers."

"Okay, sweetheart." My smiling voice tried to hide my disappointment.

"Oh, honey?"

"Yeah?" I got excited.

"I'm playing hockey with the men's team tomorrow, remember."

"Sounds good. I won't cook then. Thanks for the heads-up."

"Bye. Love you." The phone clicked.

I watered the flowers. Balanced the checkbook. Prayed for him while I ironed his shirts and watched my favorite TV show. Switched the laundry. Went to bed.

We had four fabulous vacations in one year alone. We went skiing in Colorado, to the Florida beaches and Disney World, to a cabin in northern Illinois, and to Boston, just the two of us. My family was never better. I was working for a new company in the health care field. We had moved into the perfect house. Chad and I were both making money. I knew that the neighborhood women enjoyed my husband's confidence and charm, while the guys liked his wit and humor. I had meaningful relationships with women at work and in the neighborhood. I felt lucky to have Chad as my teammate in life, every day. I was proud of the man I had married.

As the marriage grew, he became just as happy with me too. One evening, he bundled me in his arms and told me how impressed he was with the way that I had handled my new career. A tear ran down his cheek. I had never felt his respect for my work ethic; rather, I'd felt criticized for my lack of business acumen, so this was an admission of his approval in a way that let me know this was important to *him*. I had believed in him all these years.

We boated together. We daydreamed about retirement. He had his "guy time" as often as he wanted. I was never the nagging monster wife about how he spent his time, but ... over time, I did feel rejection and deep, silent hurt over it. When I was a child, my father spent time with the family. He enjoyed us. Made us a priority. This ... this was a challenge for me. But I *loved* him, still more.

In April 2002, we celebrated twelve years of marriage. Malak was in the second grade and Grace in the first grade. I was laid off from my job, and I opted to take the summer off. Chad and I took a trip without the kids, just the two of us. We sat in the sun, read books, and stayed up late talking about life plans and beach houses. We visited friends we hadn't seen in ten years, the Winstons.

To our happy surprise, the Winstons talked about their new church. This prompted further conversation between the two men, because Bill Winston had always professed to be an atheist, which made for curious discussions. Turns out that the book *The Jesus I Never Knew* had answered many questions for Bill, so Chad decided to read it. For the next four days, Chad pored over it. He loved reading on vacation. When he was done, he shared with me how much the book had helped him understand his own questions. We never discussed the specifics.

Through the years, although we went to church almost every Sunday, we rarely talked about religion. Not really any disagreements on the subject. Maybe an occasional comment on the music or the impact or context of the sermon. I made the assumption that we shared the same views, with one discrepancy—Chad's disbelief in the value of prayer still remained. I grew to value it more, having seen God answer my prayers, whether about the kids or Chad. Whether for a job, a sick parent, or a family issue, I leaned on my faith.

After renewing our romance and enjoying our private vacation to unprecedented levels, we returned home. We had it all; nothing was out of place. We made financial strides for the first time in our lives. Our children were happy, healthy, and thriving. We lived in the best neighborhood in the city, with a twenty-four–children cul-de-sac and a full calendar of social events. Our church embraced us with a place to belong as well.

On summer weekends, we drove to see both of our families, who coincidentally lived across the street from each other. Can't beat it. Both families invited us to play on their boats all day long, while eating fabulously juicy watermelons. We knew we were so blessed. In my head and in my heart, there ran a tape loop that repeated "state of grace, state of grace" continually. Strange. Yes. It was as if the words were telling me something.

Having lost my job, I had succumbed to the neighbors' pleas to stay home and spend time with my kids, if just for the summer. The nationwide layoff was not a surprise. A break in my career would look less ambitious, my father told me. When I was offered a job for twice my salary, I still turned it down. A deep, stern, internal voice was loud, saying "No." Like a loud gut instinct. "No" in such a way that I could not ignore it. I felt a sense of finality and importance about it. It was so indelible that I can still hear it, years later—no reverb, no echo, just cold and terminal. Irrevocable and non-negotiable. I waited, knowing something in my soul.

A couple of years passed in the house, establishing the kids and their friends. Malak came in the house from playing with the boys in the neighborhood and confessed that they were eating worms and peeing in the neighbors' yards. He told me that he had faked them out by pretending to eat worms and letting the others do all the watering. That was the softer side of Malak, part of his older-child, responsible personality traits shining through.

I rolled around on the floor more, wrestling with the kids. I let them stay up late since I wasn't working. I spent endless days with friends at the health club's outdoor pool and at summer barbecues. I let the kids eat Popsicles, one in each hand, before dinner, contrary to the typical strict sugar-consumption restrictions of a schedule-laden working mom.

We were vacationing on the Fourth of July in northern Illinois in a primitive cabin when Malak announced that he wanted to take a bike ride to the cemetery down the street. My husband and I looked at one another. I was more than happy to stay lakeside and play with Grace and the other families. My adventurous men rode half a mile away to indulge my son's curiosities. A graveyard. Hm-m-m.

Upon their return, I asked, "How was it?"

"Pretty cool, I guess," Chad said of our son's enthusiasm. He shrugged.

One month later, this would be far more ironic than anyone knew. A golden thread tying other small threads together was what this was. At the time, it was just … odd.

Chad took a fishing trip to Canada at the end of July. It was a warm summer night, with my bedroom windows open, when Malak crawled under the covers with me. He buried his face in my neck and said with total sincerity and sweet innocence "Mommy, I'm afraid I'm going to die." I stared at the ceiling fan turning overhead, thinking of how to comfort him.

"Oh, silly, you are hidden in the shadow of the almighty God, and you're going to be rocking with me in an old rocking chair until I am ninety years old. Don't worry." But I heard an inner voice—that whisper that I had come to know: *"You can't promise him that."*

I was alarmed by that thought. What mother would have that idea? Something was wrong. A tear ran down my face, in fear of the possible revelation of a telling wisdom that I could not understand. Confused by the twisted thoughts that contradicted the nature of my motherhood, I hugged tighter, and Malak's arms squeezed harder around my neck. The ceiling fan sent a soft breeze down on us. The long white linen drapes billowed as if they were listening. I smelled his skin and his hair. The single most memorable scent on this earth must surely be the uniquely, intoxicating soft perfume of our children. The familiar of those we love when we embrace. My little boy was draped over me in surrender, looking for comfort. I wanted to defend him from every one of his monsters. We are, after all, our children's greatest safe harbor. I said a long devoted prayer, kissed him, and put him in bed.

That was July.

In August, exhausted, on my knees next to Malak's bed, he said, "Mom, I want to help starving kids in Africa."

"Baby, you are in the second grade. God wants you to do well in the second grade, but when you get older, we can do something more, okay?"

"'kay," he conceded. He had been moved by a photo of a World Vision child we supported who was about his age.

I put my head on Malak's tummy to say the first few words of the bedtime prayers. He cupped his hands above my head. We started in unison with:

"Now I lay me down to sleep; I pray the Lord my soul to keep; if I should die before I wake, I pray the Lord my soul to take. God bless Daddy, Mommy, Gracie, and me. Thank You for health, happiness, and safety." When he whispered "amen," it tickled my ear.

With Malak done, I hurried off but was stopped at the door by … something in the corner of my line of sight. I looked back. Malak's little hands were fluttering in the air, and he was speaking inaudibly. Curious, I leaned back and asked, "What were you just doing, li'l man?"

"I was catching your words in my hands"—they had been directly above my face seconds prior—"rolling them together like this"—he rolled his hands in demonstration—"and throwing them up to God so he can hear them!" The child left me speechless. How beautiful. Who does that? How did he *think* of that?

Back in April, I had confessed to Chad that I had a dark feeling that I was unable to quell. I hesitated before saying, "We have it so good. We have the world by the tail, but I have a feeling that something bad is coming. I know you think I'm crazy, but I just have to tell you." I braced for his response. This was important. I was afraid I was going to get the "shrug off," but that's not what I got.

He said, "Really? Me too." The words *"These are the best of times; these are the worst of times"* ran through my mind.

I was caught off guard. I'd expected him to toss off my words, like he had when I worried when Grace fell from the swing set, and I thought she should see a doctor. Or the time he agreed to watch the kids when I had the annual day of Christmas shopping with the girls, but he instead went to Iowa with the boys—hunting. This response gave me more courage.

"Yeah, I think the fall is going to be hard for some reason. I don't know why." Again, he agreed, "Me too."

Having a little more leeway to say still more, I continued. "But I think you will handle it better for some reason than you would have, had you not read that book that the Winstons gave us."

"But I don't believe in prayer," he said.

I replied, "God help you that you should ever need something bigger than yourself. God help you if something happens that you can't fix by yourself. If you should ever have to learn that painful lesson under the wrath of God, I don't want to be around for it. I'm scared for both of us."

I wish I hadn't been right.

It was almost exactly a month after the bike ride to the graveyard on the North Shore. Grace's birthday party was that first week in August, with all the proper fanfare. The seven-year-old girls came fancy-dancy in their best costume dresses. I curled the girls' hair and polished their nails, as Chad played waiter/cabana boy with a tray of plastic champagne glasses filled with cherry Kool-Aid punch. They danced to their favorite music in the backyard.

A few days later, on August 5, 6, and 7, I awoke at 2:00 a.m. precisely—three nights in a row. In my thirty-something years, I'd always slept rock solid, other than if I heard one of the babies crying. I got up and went downstairs to watch TV, so as not to disturb anyone. Flipping through the channels, I came upon a woman preaching. Oddly enough, I had seen her giving the same speech earlier in the day as I flipped through the channels, but I had ignored her. This time, I had to hear her, and I knew it. She was hollering, "Just say *yes* to God, no matter what it is. There may be consequences, but God will make something great out of your life, if you say *yes!*"

"Okay, God," I said aloud. "Yes, whatever you want. Fine. I'm tired and going to bed now."

Dragging my toes up the steps, I looked in on Malak, who was talking in his sleep.

How I wish I had lingered there just a little longer.

Always trust in the still, small voice.

— CHAPTER 3 —

Thirty Seconds Can Change Your Life

August 7

I let Chad oversleep on this morning. Looking back from the bedroom door, I retraced my steps to kiss him on the forehead. Later, rifling through my desk for a printed copy of my résumé, I grabbed a long-lost CD with a song I loved. I had misplaced it for three years, but it now had appeared, a golden thread of sorts. The name of the song is "Farther than Your Grace Can Reach" by Jonathan Pierce. It's about how you are never out of arm's length from God, whether by sin or situation.

I'd had the perfect summer off, but now it was time to get back to work. I would drop the kids with my mother, as I had a job interview near her house.

On the drive there, Malak hollered, "Mom, I have to go to the bathroom!"

I stopped at a McDonald's about forty miles from home. Grace and I remained in the car while Malak went in to use the restroom. After a few seconds, anxiety grew over the thought of his safety, but he quickly returned and climbed into the minivan. Before leaving the parking lot, I called out, "Seat belts? We aren't going anywhere until I hear the seat belts!"

A tiny, rather unattractive gray bird was holding on sideways to my car's antenna as I backed out of the parking spot. *His eye is on the sparrow.* I had heard that Scripture. I knew the sparrow symbolized God's eye on his children. (A thread so unexpected, I almost could miss it.)

Exactly six minutes later, my cell phone displayed a missed call. It was from Chad, but he didn't leave a message. I dialed him back, got his voicemail, and hung up.

As I drove over the hills my eye was irritated and watering. The two-lane road was without intersections or ramps, just lined with evergreen woods on either side of this remote southern Illinois highway. There were no gas stations for miles, no restaurants, and my cruise control was set at 69 mph, four miles over the speed limit. There were no approaching cars. The closest vehicle was fifteen car-lengths in front of me. So I pulled down the visor mirror to remove this foreign article from one eye while I kept the other eye on the road.

Violently and in slow motion, my chest flew forward into the steering wheel, and my head hit the windshield, smashing it. I felt no pain. The sounds of ratcheting, scratching, screaming steel ground us to a crawl. Red covered my whole view. Blinking, I tried to define what I was looking at. I had slammed into the back of something that had dropped into my path from the sky. Smoke, dust, and the smell of burning brakes overwhelmed the fear-filled passengers in the car. I couldn't open any of the doors. All the windows were locked in position, shattered but intact. I searched desperately. To my relief, the passenger-side window was open and all the way down, free from jagged edges of glass, while the rest of the car felt like a steel box incinerator. The window was the only exit.

Grace was on the floor behind my seat, bleeding from the mouth and unconscious. I went to pass her out of the window as I wept and prayed, "Lord, take care of my baby girl." An angelic-like presence standing at the door said, "Yes, Lord." Where had *he* come from? Looking back at Malak, he appeared to be free from injury, not a scratch on him.

"Are you okay, baby?"

"Yes," he groaned, still in his seatbelt.

"Can you get out, honey? We need to get out of the car."

My voice was sweet but shaking with alarm, as I pictured us burning alive. Just as I was fearing suffocation, air and light flooded the car, and a hand reached for mine, helping me jump out from the vehicle. An EMT. My knees hurt on the leap down. I sat roadside in the gravel. Grace lay next to me, screaming, her teeth jagged, blood running from her mouth. EMTs shouted out vitals and recorded them. I looked behind me for Malak, but the other EMTs had taken him twenty-five feet away from us to the roadside. I tried calming Grace down with my hand on her head. I had to stay sane and concentrate. Sirens blared. People were throwing questions at us.

I had to call Chad. "We were in an accident," I blurted.

"Is everyone okay?"

"Yeah, I think so. Grace is bleeding out of her mouth. Malak seems okay. They are working on him …"

"Send them to Memorial Hospital. I will go there now," he insisted.

"Okay. I have to go. I love you. I'm sorry. I think I totaled the car."

Loud noises. Gawkers. Distractions. Grace's screaming. Malak appeared gray for some reason. I looked back at the car. It was latched on to a dump truck's bumper—an overloaded, gravel-filled truck. A tall, skinny man approached in jeans and a T-shirt—the truck driver, I supposed.

"I'm sorry, but where did you come from?" I asked.

"From that road back there. From the gravel pit."

"Where? There's no on-ramp or road marker, no street sign, or merge lane. Where would you enter? I don't understand. I was watching."

"I was slow gettin' started and loaded down, so you missed me 'til all the cars had passed around me," he replied. "I saw you coming up on my bumper."

I knew in my heart that every mom has been distracted while driving, holding a bottle to her baby in the backseat or trying to grab a pacifier when her infant cried, but I threw my culpability down like the loser's hand at poker and conceded at that moment that it was all my fault. How could I have done this?

The policeman asked, "Your name? What's your address, ma'am? The kids' names? Their ages? Any allergies? Are you injured? What is your husband's name? What happened? Can I get your insurance information? Do you want them airlifted to Memorial. We have two helicopters making their way, but it will take some time."

I tried to focus on providing the correct answers, but between fire trucks and ambulances, it was hard.

Strapped down on stretchers with Grace strapped next to me, screaming uncontrollably, I heard a woman say, "Talk to her, Mom." We couldn't see each other, but I reached for my daughter's hand. "It's okay, Gracie. Mommy is right here. Don't worry. Mommy's right here."

It wasn't until then that I began to cry. The female EMT encouraged me. "Keep talking, Mom." It was like medicine for my fried nerves. I unscrambled my brain.

Holding back the tears, I sang, "Winnie the Pooh. Winnie the Pooh. Tubby little cubby all stuffed with fluff. He's Winnie the Pooh. Winnie the Pooh. Silly, willy-nilly old bear." Then, using the same tune, I sang, "'Mommy loves Grace. Daddy loves Grace. Everybody in the world loves Grace. Mommy loves Grace. Daddy loves Grace. Silly, willy-nilly all day.' You're going to be okay. Don't cry, honey. Don't cry."

We reached the closest small-town clinic; it was too quiet. I didn't see either Malak or Grace. No noise from the hallway. No information. I was waiting to hear the helicopter blades. I waited. And waited.

The sputter of the helicopter on the rooftop arrived as I was being wheeled in for X-rays. The nurse said, "Maybe you want to say something to Malak. He's leaving now. Tell him you love him, if you want? I don't know if he'll hear you, and I know you can't see him, but you can yell to him if you'd like. It's okay."

So with every ounce of breath I had left, straining my throat, I yelled, "I love you Malak!" It echoed in the sterile room and down a dark empty hall. I wanted to be with him, near him, holding his hand, though I never heard the smallest peep from that hall.

Two soft-spoken nurses came over and offered to pray with me, each taking one of my hands. In the health care field, I knew they were not typically allowed to do that. While they prayed, I mumbled *yes* through whimpers of fear and gratitude. One nurse looked at me and said, "The second helicopter arrived. Grace is leaving." I sighed in relief.

The small-town staff, the EMTs, and rescue teams trickled into every doorway. Their faces looked pale and somber. What did they know that I didn't?

I sat despondent, in shock, and hauntingly unattached. The nurses ran in and out, talking among themselves over lab results. In the emptiness, I recounted the things that I was grateful for. I was grateful I had not been on the phone while driving or, worse yet, singing along to the CD and not paying attention. I relived the moments of the day—kissing Chad, jumping out to check on Malak, the smile on Grace's face. The road in front of me and the split second that changed my life, while trying to get that one eyelash out of my eye. Silent on the inside, I waited for answers. I asked myself the first of many questions. Then the phone rang. The nurse handed it to me.

"When will you *be* here?" Chad asked with urgency.

"Mom is on her way, but it could be another hour."

"Malak stopped breathing three times. He's been in cardiac arrest, and they're going to do surgery to see what the problem is. They ... don't think it looks good."

The phone fell from my clammy fingers and clattered on the tile floor. The Middle Eastern doctor approached my bedside, lowered his calming voice, and uttered, "I can tell you're a woman of faith. Hold onto that. Use that. You will be okay." He patted my arm.

Bewildered, I whispered, "Thank you." What was he *saying*?

My mom arrived, but we didn't speak much. She assured me that this would be all right in the end, but I fell unusually quiet. Numbness crept into my belly. With a patella fracture, I sat crosswise on the leather backseat of her silver BMW, crutches on my lap, for the long ride to Memorial Hospital.

Arriving at the ER, a wheelchair delivered us expediently to a private door. And behind it, curled up on his back in the corner of the room, holding his arms around his stomach, was Chad. I knew instinctively, as the bottom fell out of my heart, what I could not intellectually comprehend.

Chad's red-faced, devastated, indescribable emotions could not push his breath out to speak. My regret and guilt first germinated at that second, in that dark, black soil.

"He ... died." Chad mouthed the words, with air flowing from his lips. Like hot lava erupting, my shrieking and sobbing boiled over, stinging my face and burning my soul. Hugging himself in agony, Chad's veins popped in his neck and brow. He looked as if he was in an invisible straitjacket, unable to breathe, detached and unraveling.

From my wheelchair, begging a look from my pastor, who had crouched down next to me, large tears ran off his face. He glanced away in his attempt to retain his composure.

"*Noooooooooooo!*" I rocked back and forth in my wheelchair. Chad still rolled in anguish, overwhelmed by his misery. We didn't hug. I couldn't hobble over to him. It was so all-consuming—the three of us in the small, cold room with nothing but a blood-red leather bench.

We were led into Malak's hospital room. My husband and I were left there alone with our dreams—or rather, without them. Malak was truly a magnificent boy. Now, nothing lay there but a familiar precious form, yet paradoxically alien. Watching Chad's face, his body language, and seeing the devastation of the unquenchable love of my life in such torment because of my unredeemable hand was a double-bladed sword. In that moment, I realized that I was the murderer of two people. My own agony had a rhythm like childbirth, unprepared for the next contraction and each one more severe and intense than the last. I didn't get to hold Malak's hand, like so many other times in his life. Or Chad's. We were isolated in our own shock.

As if outside of myself, I watched Chad as he stood like a statue. Sunken shoulders. Rippling pain spread across his face. Stiff arms. A tendon in his jaw pulsed in distress. We were poised on either side of the bed in the kind of silence that only death can deliver. We tried not to speak or cry, but the dam broke. He hung like a caged gorilla, swaying as he held on to the bed rails. I had never imagined this. The weight of his anger rushed through the room like a tornado. He stopped to cradle lifelessness in his arms, as if afraid to remember the painful magnitude of what it represented in life, while in fear of forgetting one miniscule detail or memory. I, the murderer, came here to say good-bye. Immediately, I realized I had killed not just one love, but two. Overwhelmed. Yes. I had come to say good-bye. But I had not prepared for Chad's emotional devastation, which transfixed me.

We held ourselves up, one on each side of the bed. Our knees buckled, slipping to the floor in ceaseless sobs, hanging from those railings. Seeing Chad at eye level under the raised surgical bed was like living beneath the life we had known, buried and suffocating in grief. We couldn't handle it.

Once composed, we said a few short words to each other about Malak's front teeth being crooked and cute, about his gorgeous white hair and long lashes, and his little hands. Jesus, I hope we never lose the image of those little hands that had hugged nine hundred times. Images flashed in my head—Malak as a baby, with a bottle, playing with my hair as he fell asleep in my gaze. His kisses.

"You can look at his chest incision, if you want to," Chad said.

But that seemed ridiculous. I would not see my baby again until he lay in a casket.

A death or loss was instead intended to give birth to something indescribably valuable, that you would not possess, perceive, or obtain, were it any other way but by that specific experience.

CHAPTER 4

Good-Bye

It's shameful to admit that we hadn't seen Grace in hours and that we didn't notice how much time had passed. How would we tell her? When Chad and I arrived in her ER room, her intuition told her that something was wrong. In her own anxiety and pain, she began to cry. She was mostly sedated, lying in a neck brace, with her mouth torn and bloodstained. The chief resident, who, unfortunately, also accidentally removed a permanent tooth when he treated Grace's shattered lower jaw, disappointed us. But Grace was alive, so we celebrated. Of course, no one would admit to fault for legal reasons, but I was in no position to place blame for human error.

"Where's Malak?" Grace asked, her voice hoarse. I stared at her, selecting thoughts and words. Nothing would come out. "What?" she asked wide-eyed.

Chad pointed to the ceiling, resting his head on his arm with disappointment. "He di ..." His voice trailed off.

Observing Chad was like pouring alcohol on my gaping wound of a conscience. What had I done? How did this happen? The nurse arrived with more IV sedation for Grace. We hugged and kissed her, leaving her to her coma-like sleep. I envied her temporary escape.

My mascara met my chin and my lipstick had migrated to my forehead. I wiped my face with dirty palms. I made tired, bland decisions about everything. At times, I felt falsely courageous and even superhuman, while conversely a shell of myself, driven to self-infliction as a means of punishment, leading then to denial altogether.

People flooded into the hospital. The Johnsons, Caroline and Ryan, arrived, along with other friends from Chad's work. Caroline and Chad had been on the same finance department team for about six years. I had met Ryan maybe a couple of times—a very nice couple, genuine and kind. Our family arrived from the Midwest region, having driven all night long, as well as friends from Colorado and across the nation. The depth of friendships and family love washed over us in awe and comfort.

My best friend, Sutton, and her husband, Ty, drove hours from Wisconsin. I met her eyes across the room, and we hugged in unspoken lament. As little girls, we had dreamed of perfect weddings, jobs, and children. Never this.

Chad's mom and dad arrived next. I almost couldn't look at them. The magnitude of hurt on their faces pricked my guilt reflex even further. Her puffy eyes were evidence of her hours of tears.

I didn't want to know, but I *had* to know what had killed Malak. People were asking already. I would have to answer those questions. Was he was wearing his seatbelt? How did he actually die?

"Malak was brain dead and ischemic, spleen and liver severed in half, femoral artery to the lower extremities detached," the surgeon explained.

I felt myself shutting down as he described in graphic detail what my distraction had wrought. My shortness of breath was followed by dizziness as I white-knuckled the arms of the chair.

"Five percent of seatbelt injuries are due to 'deceleration injuries'—the organs hit each other on impact, causing injury, due to the restraint device at impact on the abdomen," the surgeon went on. "He bled to death internally. Typically, the patient dies within minutes. It was a miracle that Malak reached the hospital."

So the seatbelt, the thing that should have saved him, played a role in his death.

I had to have air. Sucking up an entire room, I barreled out to the waiting room, past the crowded hall, and raced toward the exit sign.

A house full of guests made the morning of the funeral more manageable. Chad's parents were in the guest room. His brothers were in the family room. My mom slept on the floor of Grace's room. People were ironing in the kitchen, and there was a line for the bathroom. Chad's mom had gone to the store, and I could smell breakfast cooking all the way upstairs.

I woke up staring at Chad. I welcomed the noise in the house. We brushed our teeth without a word. I looked over at him, hoping to connect. He glared back, looked into the sink, and spit.

Grace called with excitement, "Mom! Come here! Come *here*!" I ran into her room. Still in her pink pj's, with my best girlfriend, Sutton, sitting next to her, she squealed "Mom! Pennies! Do you see them? I woke up to this pile of pennies in my bed!" Looking down, there were indeed eight to ten pennies in her bed.

"Where did they come from?" I asked.

"Pennies are from heaven," Sutton smiled. "Didn't you know that?"

"Not really …" I confessed.

"Pennies are evidence that someone is thinking of you in heaven!" Sutton exclaimed.

Wide-eyed and bewildered, we all looked at each other.

The master bedroom was a different environment. I walked into our huge closet to find Chad, his two brothers, and his parents. They were carrying him, his arms around their shoulders, dragging him out of the closet as my mountain of a man crumbled from the earthquake within.

"I … can't … decide what to wear to my … s-s-s-son's funeral." He collapsed.

Silence fell. Every face pursed, waiting for the next word to break the tension. Suffering grievously, we all showed signs of shaking limbs and trembling lips.

"Wear whatever you want to, honey," Chad's mom said so beautifully.

"I don't know. Maybe something green," he said, still staring at the floor.

"Perfect." She smiled. "That's perfect, dear."

My knees bent, and I feared I would fall to the floor myself. I looked over to my mom, groping for relief in our unsustainable atmosphere. "I … I … I can't, Mama."

Lovingly, she cupped her hands to the sides of my cheeks like a horse's blinders, blocking my view of anyone in the room. Pressing her tough stare and nose to mine, she said, "We … can … do … this. Okay, baby? We can do this."

I studied her. Looking at me with a lionness's bold confidence, she willed strength into me. She shut out the world for a moment. It worked.

Somehow, we all arrived at the funeral parlor at eleven o'clock. There would be a fifteen-minute graveside burial at three, and the funeral at the church at three thirty. We did this all in one day, partly because the funeral home was busy and partly because I couldn't have my son dead on a cold slab for nearly a week. I wanted to make it all go away—just get Malak buried and deal with the rest of the mess inside of us later.

The visitation involved children laughing and writing notes, drawing pictures to Malak as if he were simply away on vacation. Grace made a handful and placed them in the casket. I would steal a peek from across the room between brief lags in conversations. I was afraid. After everyone left, I mustered the courage to approach the forbidden zone. I wanted time with my son by myself when no one would see me become the crazy woman.

My eyes traced the green casket first. I warmed up to the idea. Malak's favorite color. Man-sized, because a child's casket was too short for his tall frame at eight years old. I guess they only make a couple of sizes. *You have to look.* Perfect in his hockey jersey and khaki shorts; he would have hated a suit. His face was calm and his hair pushed to the side in the most natural way. I saw the *one* love letter that I had written him a few weeks prior, exposed to everyone's view:

> *Dear Baby Malak,*
> *I am so very proud of you. You make my heart smile. I love you faster than a cheetah, bigger than the moon, and more than the meanest storm. I love you so much my heart hurts. You are funny, silly, so smart, and precious to your mom and dad. I will love you forever and ever.*
> *XOXO*
> *Mommy*

He had been so pleased by that note that he had taped it to the headboard of his bed. I realized then how sad it was that I had not written more love letters. Sometimes, the most significant things are the small ones. This note gave me peace, and I was so thankful that I had listened to the still small voice to write it in the busy errands of the day that day. His blanket and favorite now-dirty white bear were there. I had sewn up the neck and bleached him time after time. The flowers surrounding Malak were massive, overwhelming me with their aroma, juxtaposed with the nauseating blunt reality of the moment.

My heart raced. A pulsing pain rose. What I had forced back was coming out; my pounding fist pummeled the edge of the casket in defiance. I wanted the boy back from where ... he was not. He seemed here but not really. The intangible familiarity of him seemed near but *not*. Groaning in anger, I managed to concede, "It's not going to be okay, Malak. It's never going to be okay."

This darkness scared me, but I ran from the edge, the guilt, and the denial that came with it. I gritted my teeth. Committed to make "good" come from this, I vowed to be a sane, strong woman, instead of a wilted, overly whiny, repulsive, pathetic one. I would swallow my poison and live with it in my veins for this lifetime.

My armpits were sore from my crutches, and my eyes burned even with sunglasses. I had feared this, most of all. I couldn't deal with the cemetery, and I knew it. I had mentally avoided the burial experience for two days.

The wonderful man who married us, Pastor George, performed the graveside service and per our request, it was expedient. His face, his humor, and his deep remorse were evident; somehow, it united us all. I didn't listen. I left. Checked out. Chad handed flowers to us all to place on the coffin. *Will I vomit?* I looked at the sky and then at Pastor George's handsome tie. I looked at the ground near the casket. I saw the sinkhole peeking from behind the tarp that would suck my baby away, like the arms of the dead, grabbing him. *Wow. That was a bizarre image.* I seemed to have scary hallucinations about death. Chad's dad placed his rose, pulling me out of my daydream. My own father followed suit, profoundly protective and lovingly resigned as he touched the coffin. I don't remember placing a rose. We carpooled to the church, relieved to have survived emotionally.

From the back of the sanctuary, I saw the pews filled with people. I refused to look around. Guarding my composure, I wore the "blinders" my mom had placed on me that morning. I was numb and irretrievable, even in this sea of love. The piano prelude began. We walked down to the front, feeling the love and their eyes on us. Chad's mom leaned over and whispered to us, "Grace is sitting on the front steps with Sutton. They are talking and playing. That's okay, right?" We exchanged looks, nodding. "That's good. Sure, " I said. I hadn't even noticed she wasn't with us.

Pastor Steve welcomed the congregation, but all the way from the pulpit, his sorrowful, blue eyes met mine. Kate, his beautiful wife, who had always complimented my singing, hugged Chad and me as we sat down.

Over the years, they loved us with great grace, laughter, and honesty. I shut out all sound after that: the sniffles in the crowd, the intensity of the music. Chad and I didn't speak or look at each other throughout the majority of the service, except to hold hands for a moment, like brave soldiers marching toward the fortress.

"Let us read the family creed," Pastor Steve declared. Looking down at the program, I saw the cover read "The Family Creed."

"Oh, honey, that's so perfect," I whimpered. How that kissed my soul. I had chosen the song I loved and I had sung it countless times myself, but now it was so much more intimate. About the beauty of children, the changes in life as we grow old, and when God calls us home. I had sung professionally over the years, so it was cruel punishment that I couldn't sing it *now*. I think Chad and the family felt it would be too difficult for me. It was my last gift to him. A girl from the church that had a voice that I loved stood in my place. As the music played, I held my breath until her first word. I could sing this in my sleep, and I wanted it perfect.

Pastor Steve spoke. "What would Malak say to us today? He would say that he is happy in heaven. Faith was easy for Malak. He worried about starving children in Africa and wanted to bring them toys. He was kind to everyone. The worst thing I could dig up about him was that he ate a worm, and as it turned out, he spit it out. Malak was a very social child, nice to everyone. His Sunday school teacher said he was always smiling. He didn't need anyone to entertain him. He made boats and planes out of tin foil, plastic odds and ends, and paper clips. Dad was his best friend."

Pausing for composure, Pastor Steve then told the story of Horatio Spafford, who penned "It Is Well with My Soul" after the death of his son, the loss of all his financial holdings in a company fire in Chicago, and later, the drowning deaths at sea of his wife and four daughters. He had intended to join them on the ship but stayed back for a business meeting and sent them on ahead. How discouraged and empty he must have felt. Yet even then, Spafford sang, it is well with his soul. "Let us all join in now and sing this song."

What an inspired vision of pronounced character and a call to courage. I raised my right arm to the sky and closed my eyes, facing the cyclone of pain with something near gratitude. Tears showered my face for the last chorus. Belting it out, I tried to choose a harmony part as a love song to

Malak. I sang with my heart, cracking loudly, the most beautiful sound I could make as an offering to both my son and my Savior.

Pastor Steve's closing statement was, "Give yourself the gift of knowing that you were the best parents you could have been." There was nowhere to go from here but up. I laughed to myself. This was the worst of life.

Write more love notes; blow more kisses. Write your own personal/family creed. It may be of great significance for you. It is sure to be a golden thread of sorts, describing your impact on the world.

CHAPTER 5

Obsessions

Things that make you feel better: booze, sex, shopping. Happy hour visited our house *every day* at 3:30 p.m. for weeks after the funeral. Alcohol, however, wasn't the sedative I had hoped for. It diminished my self-esteem and increased my depression. Chad's therapy was Belvedere vodka in a tall glass, on the rocks, with a splash of raspberry vodka for the good-night kiss.

There wasn't much conversation in our house either. I wondered if Chad would forgive me. We did the best we could to cope. I had obliterated the life we had loved. I believed his coping skills deserved my complete grace. I, after all, had done this.

We whispered in the dark, both staring at the ceiling, night after night, absorbing our own experiences. Would we ever know what our old life felt like? In bottomless penance, I held his hand under the covers, wept quiet tears, and frantically repeated, "I'm sorry, I'm sorry, I'm sorry, I'm sorry ..." thirty times or more. Breathing through whispers and a spillage of quiet, ceaseless sobs, I added, "For the rest of our lives and past forever, I am so, so sorry." I didn't know how to begin to apologize.

Chad responded beautifully. "That's something you will have to find peace with for yourself."

Trees were donated to our yard, the schoolyard, and a nearby park. A school bench was painted green and installed in Malak's honor. Letters, prayers, faxes, and calls poured in. And food; I didn't cook for three months. Plus there was an additional three months of restaurant dinner gift certificates, all arranged by the church and our neighbors. I muttered something selfish about wanting Malak's birthstone in a ring and almost immediately, a friend purchased one and delivered it to my door. How loved we were. One hour at a time, these people saved us.

I heard that a boy the same age as Malak gave a speech for a school project in Kansas City on the proper use of seat belts and booster seats. Malak was seventy-six pounds. The booster seats are supposed to be used until the weight of eighty pounds. It helps to elevate the child's hips so that the seatbelt rides lower on the abdomen, near the hip bones, for better protection of the internal organs in an accident. If I had made him use one, he might be alive today.

Word got out, and the local DMV held safety clinics to check the child-seat restraints to ensure their proper fit. Parents hugged their kids and renewed a commitment to each other. Our loss meant awareness so that other families might be spared our experience.

One day from the kitchen window, I watched the neighborhood children congregate in our backyard. They let off green helium balloons into the sky with handwritten messages to Malak attached to the strings. Wow. They had come up with the idea that they would all stand on a large plaque given as a gift that read: "If tears could build a stairway and memories a lane, I'd walk right up to heaven and bring you back again." I found a few pebbles in Grace's dresser drawers on which she had inscribed "I love you, Malak" in permanent marker.

For the first few weeks, I opened my eyes in the morning, rolled to my side, and smelled the pillow. It was far more enticing than the stench of another day. Queasy, I'd reach over to the nightstand for a dissolvable Pepcid. I contemplated breakfast with little enthusiasm. A shower was a required practice, but I chose not to wear any makeup. Roughly three months passed before the morning nausea did too.

Our friend, Sutton, unbeknownst to me, had extracted Malak's dirty clothes from the laundry, folding them and placing them in his room, so that the scent of him would linger. Though she never mentioned it, it was a precious gesture. Smelling Malak's sheets or his favorite pajamas helped soothe me. I promised myself I would stop being ridiculous tomorrow or the next day. I only went into his room when missing him was greater than the pain of remembering.

In the closet hung his other hockey jersey, number four, with signatures from his teammates and coaches, gifted as a surprise keepsake after his death. A purple tissue-paper–wrapped box on the top shelf was left for us to open one day when we were ready, to "help" us with the grief process. I wasn't ready. I just looked at it. A medal, his skates and pads in a sports bag next to his pajamas were all still on the floor of his closet. I looked down near the pajamas and found a penny. I smiled. The phone rang.

"How are you today?" my mother asked.

I fidgeted. "Hi, Mom. It's a hard day."

"I was thinking of a couple funny things to share with you. I was thinking about how you struggled with yourself so much over not taking that job, but everything worked out for the best, under the circumstances."

"It was better than a winning million-dollar lottery ticket, Mom."

"How's Grace?"

"She seems oddly fine at home. She's in school all day. I'm relieved she doesn't see me cry much. She's playing with friends too. I was cleaning in the family room, and I found Pop-Tarts and peanut M&M's stashed in the side cushion of Chad's recliner. Chad says he finds them there all the time, I had no idea. Malak must have hidden the treats in the chair while watching cartoons."

"I was remembering the time that you came and picked the kids up when we thought I had hurt the family jewels!" Mom tossed into the conversation.

We giggled some more. From there it was easy. Easy to just close my eyes and remember the story, like a movie playing in my mind, so real and alive. My mom often babysat the kids.

"When I picked them up from your house," I said, "you answered the door and put your hand over your mouth, and you said, 'I fear Malak may have hurt the family jewels today!' Laughter erupted from me. "You looked so nervous, Mom!"

"And you ... looked so confused as to how this could happen!" Mom laughed. "When that mean, heavy toilet seat fell on his little pee-pee, and I heard the saddest yelping *yowch* from the bathroom"—we belly laughed—"it sounded so awful. I worried it was permanently bruised or bent."

"I was afraid to tell Chad, so I brought him to Jack, the family nurse practitioner. He was hilarious about the whole thing. He asked Malak to pull his pants down and he said, 'Malak, I heard ... is it true that you have *three peckers?*"

"Malak didn't get the joke," Mom squealed.

"After we got done with the checkup, Jack said to Malak, 'Don't worry;

it's not gonna fall off'!" Then I added, "Oh, such a nice man, Jack and his family."

"Yes. He's funny, *just* when you need it."

"Oh, Mom. Then I was remembering the horrible time I pinned him to the ground, yelling at him, only to fall off next to him and apologize for my anger. I pledged never to do it again, which prompted the love letter that was posted at the funeral. That's the irony of the letter. Mom, I … think about that now."

"I know, honey." She spoke softly. "I loved reading the *I Love You Forever* book that I bought." She began singing, "'I'll love you forever, I'll like you for always, as long as I'm living, my baby, you'll be.' That's how I feel about you too, baby girl."

"Thanks, Mama. I love you," I whispered.

"I'm gonna let you go."

"Mom?"

"Yes?"

"Chad wants the biggest car we can afford to replace the totaled van. He wants a car that won't even *fit* in the garage. We'd have to take out the back stairs, and it still might not fit. That's crazy talk. We've been fighting over it. I think we agreed on a Suburban, which *will* fit in the garage. What if I ever hit and killed someone else with this huge piece of metal? I know he wants to protect us, but I could kill a whole family in that thing. I will freak out if I so much as dent it parking in my own garage."

"One day at a time."

"Y—love you. We are going to a work party tonight. The Johnsons, the Wilsons, McInerys, Jacksons, and Maloys. They have all been so incredible to us. I couldn't repay them. I don't know how we would have survived. Great food. We laugh. All the kids play."

"You need to do that. Love you, love you, love you," she sang.

I obsessed over the truck while cooking the mac 'n' cheese. I agonized over it for days, nervously running my finger across my lower lip in contemplation. It was my desire to resolve the accident from a logical standpoint. Telling no one, I put a box of tissues in the Taurus and drove forty minutes to the accident site.

Rolling up over the hill, I watched for any hint of a road on the right side where a large truck could enter my lane of the highway. I drove past it and saw nothing. Nothing? Befuddled, I took a right at the first opportunity after the crash site.

I spied a small stand-alone house, hidden in a cul-de-sac. I drove up to it and rang the bell. A young mother answered cautiously.

"Hi, please forgive me," I said in a rush, "but I am looking for a gravel pit somewhere near here. It's really important to me. Could you help? Just south of here, is there a road that meets this intersection that is related to a gravel yard?"

"No, not that I'm aware of. I'm sorry," she said.

"Thank you," I conceded in my irritated desperation, feeling betrayed. *How could a woman who lives less than nine hundred feet from the scene of the accident not know of a huge gravel pit here?*

Crossing the road to return home, on a whim I stopped at the butcher shop, across the highway from the tire marks left by the wreck. I sat in the car staring absently at the dashboard. This was so vital for my peace. They *must* know something. I swung open the car door.

Behind the tall butcher's case, I asked the clerk, my voice shaking and my breath staggered, "I was wondering … is there a gravel pit across the way?"

"Yeah, why?" he said curiously, smiling.

"And is there a road that comes out of nowhere, just south of here on the northbound side?" He looked confused. He was going to ask another question, and I think I was afraid of it, so I quickly said, "My son died there recently, and I just *need* to know. Please."

"Um, let me get the owner, Mr. Nelson." He disappeared in the back. When he returned, he resumed wrapping meat behind the counter, saying, "He'll be out in a minute."

"Thanks," I whispered.

I looked like a nervous would-be bank robber—agitated, pacing, and murmuring to myself. I patted my sticky palms on my pants and straightened my shoulders before I looked up. Walking toward me was a tall, thin man, probably fifty-five, with salt-and-pepper hair and dimples.

"I made the first 911 call when I heard the accident out front. I was the first EMT on the scene of your accident, ma'am."

Limp knees. "Oh-h-h … tha-a-n-n-k you!" I hugged him, which made him a little uncomfortable. I wasn't ready for this, and judging from the tears in his eyes and the way he fidgeted with his fingers, he wasn't either.

"Please tell me *where* that road is. I have no idea where the truck came from. I never saw him, and there's no road there." I held back my words, my breath … everything. I made him walk me out to the street and show me, precisely. As he pointed across the road, I saw a wall of trees so thick it obscured anything behind it.

"If you drive past that area again, you will see an unmarked road come out right about where that tall tree stands, just south over there. Drive slow; you will see it."

With the push of spilling sadness, I asked, "Tell me, please, please. Do you know if Malak had his seatbelt on?"

"I saw on his abdomen some bruising consistent with a seatbelt in a strip across his belly."

"*Thank you.* You don't know what you did for me. I made him put it on. You couldn't know. I couldn't sleep at night because I knew—you just helped me sleep. Thank you."

"I'm sorry for your loss. That was a tough accident. Hard for even us EMTs to see. Most of us got counseling for that one."

With my cheeks dripping wet, I thanked him yet again. I got in my car, my hands still sweating. I circled on the highway one more time, this time with less traffic, pulled onto the margin, and inched slowly forward.

And oh, my stars in heaven, there it was! An old, unmarked, unpaved, single-lane road with grass growing through it. If the gravel truck was loaded with gravel, it typically used a conveyor belt to load the truck. Only barely visible from this direction was the road, yet the conveyor belt was undetectable. No streetlight. No street sign. No curb. Surely nothing was back there. No wonder *no one* knew it was there.

The closer I got, the more I examined it, and the more my body shook—those strange anxiety responses I tried to control. The harder I tried, the worse I hyperventilated, with flashes of pent-up memories. I sank into the steering wheel. Couldn't breathe. Too much.

Calm down. Pep talk yourself. "Come on, it's okay. You are fine. Get it together, woman. Start the car and drive."

I told Chad everything. He did not struggle with it; he actually seemed a little callous. This was an epiphany for me. My explanation. At least now I understood where the truck had come from. The mystery was solved for me. Why wouldn't he want to know how it happened?

The following day, I went into Malak's room, sprawled on his bed, and cried as hard as I could. It was loud, obnoxious, and uninhibited, but I couldn't rid myself of the emptiness, of the crude garbage within. After ten outrageous minutes, I was spent. Unfortunately, the process of pain-purging remained. Snapshots remained. Bitter and sweet intertwined. I looked for systematic methods to erase my circumstances and move on, save the family, and redeem myself. I couldn't cry enough, or linger in misery, or sit on the bed for years. I couldn't really die to relieve myself. What would that accomplish? And there was Grace to think of.

In the midst of my crisis, Chad strode into Malak's room.

"Do you want to go buy a big-screen TV?" he asked.

I laughed hysterically.

Booze. Sex. Shopping. Not so much the answer, unfortunately. I tried, really I did.

CHAPTER 6

Why?

We bought a fifty-something-inch TV and a forty-something-inch TV. Temporary filler. Consumption satisfaction. The rudeness of reality slapped me with a glimpse of his sock from beneath the dryer.

Why did this happen? I had time to process and ask. The beginning of normal was different now. Attending a church service was like standing naked among the parishioners. Strangers nodded when I walked by. Because they knew. My emotions were so close to the surface that I continually had to shove them down. The music was beautiful and sickening. Gratitude and surrender in worship battled for position against poisonous anger, and the start of questions for God, and of course, grief. What if I burst into spontaneous panic or unstoppable emotions? Become embarrassed and ashamed? I would plan my escape. Just get up with composure and walk to the rear doors. I would take one service at a time.

One particular Sunday, the Pastor showed a foreign film clip with subtitles put to music. It was about a father who worked on a railroad line. In one scene, an emergency up ahead on the line forced the railroad lineman to switch the high-speed train track to another track in order to avoid a collision that would kill all the passengers on the train. When lineman got the call instructing him to do so, he realized he had sent his eleven-year-old son to switch the track for the regular route, four hundred feet away. In order to save all the members on the train, his own son would be sacrificed to die for the greater good.

I watched as the son stood so obediently, waiting for his father's approval. The orchestra swelled as the music played faster, as the train moved closer and closer to the switching post. The small boy called out repeatedly to his father, waving his arms for instructions. The father's fear wouldn't let him answer. All he could do was wave his arms toward him frantically, his face streaming with passionate tears. He was powerless. The son, trusting the father. The powerlessness. The close-up on the father's face was too much for me. He was going to watch the death of his son, who trusted him implicitly.

The congregation was squirming in their seats in anticipation of the outcome. I looked down in the pew to see my hands curling so hard that my own nails were digging into my legs. My toes were on their tips, pounding into the floor in anxious unison. Totally unaware of the tension inside until I looked down, I desperately tried not to overly empathize, so I just dug my nails in deeper, hoping to cause some sort of pain that would take my mind off the moment. *Please, let this pass. … Please make this be over.* I kept repeating this to myself, but the floodgates had been opened. When I caught myself rocking, the panic had arrived. I stood up, like I had promised myself, and sprinted to the bathroom where it was safe. The tears came pouring out when I hit the sacred bathroom stall, hugging it as if it would comfort me.

How had I gotten here? Had I been criminally negligent in some way? How could God let this happen to a Christian church-going family? Wasn't he supposed to protect us? Malak wasn't ever in trouble. He was always so gentle and polite. He never went to sleep or ate dinner without saying prayers, which were always "God bless Mommy, Daddy, Gracie, and me. Thank you for health, happiness, and safety." Doesn't the Bible say He is close to little children? Didn't He hear him? The more I thought about it, the angrier I got.

As I sat in the clinic lobby for a follow-up on my knee injury, a woman next to me volunteered information that her son had been in twenty-one surgeries, costing more than a million dollars out of pocket. My eyes watered. Surely, I would have killed myself trying to save my son, day after day, heartache after heartache.

Someone told me a story of how a child was riding a bike, and the rear side mirror on a moving car hit him as the driver passed. Miraculously, the next passing car was a physician, who used a pen casing to do an emergency tracheotomy in the child's neck, and he lived.

I was angry. I decided that my faith in God should have won me something. Why believe if God couldn't answer my prayers? Without it, He was pointless. There was no hope if God let me down.

I felt like a puppet. Betrayed by the God I had tried to live right for. I had married as a virgin. I didn't cheat on taxes. I hardly missed church and gave to the poor. I prayed every day, all day, all my years. I raised my kids in Sunday school and prayed at the dinner table. I quoted Scriptures, had taken numerous Bible studies, and had gone on mission trips. What was the point? God had left me here, empty-handed. What had I done that was so horrible that I deserved the crap knocked out of me by the God in whom I had always believed and *trusted*? Where was my mercy message? Where were His loving arms? Where were His miracles?

I hated most that I had been singing praise in the car right before the accident. Why didn't God warn me with intuition, like so many other times in life? Why had Malak died in a seatbelt, and Grace lived without one? Why had I hit the man in front of me, going only fifteen miles an hour faster than he was, only to kill someone in the farthest seat back? Why? Why didn't God save Malak? He could have become a minister, a father, a husband—led a well-lived life. What good could possibly come from his extinction?

I didn't have any dreams left. I never asked for fame or fortune. I never expected a perfect life, just a normal one. Family of four, a dog, the ability to pay our bills, a solid marriage, and our health. That was all I wanted. Didn't everyone want that?

I had always made solid decisions, according to Scripture. The formula for basic success was to be intelligent about your life choices. I had been responsible. I was obsessed with the right "blessed path" inside God. I didn't believe in swearing, but now it didn't matter. If God was going to punish me, *who cared*? I laughed so hard my stomach hurt—an outburst to the insanity of my questions. Consider me devastated, obliterated, confused, and rejected. I was betrayed, severely punished, embarrassed, and crucified. I would smoke and curse and throw things. No one could judge me. I would cry until I felt better. I would skip laundry, showers, and eating. I didn't have to keep it together any longer, and for the first time in my life, I didn't want to. I didn't have to be perfect, proper, prayerful, polite, or presentable. It was all total and utter bull.

Late one night, when everyone was sleeping, I crossed the threshold into Malak's room. In a whisper, so as not to wake the rest of the house, I yelled at God. He had better show up now. He owed me. *Tell me why I should believe, God? Tell me something. Anything.* But all I got was quiet, emptiness, and the worst kind of silence. It was like a best friend who knows you're useless when you're angry. I was potentially too wounded and furious to hear what God might say, no matter how amazing. It would never make Malak's death any better. Ever.

Reaching for my Bible on the floor, I laid my head on it. It seemed aimless, nothing to give, and nothing left to get. I was done. My tears began to flow, falling onto the green cover. I was too tired to move and too devastated to care. I scrutinized my arm. What if that had been *my* arm in the casket? I would feel better. *Why didn't You take me? I would have died for him, God. Why didn't You let me?* I sobbed for real this time, unable to find an end to my misery. When I finally exhausted myself and was completely spent, I pondered how Chad would have raised the children if I had died. I worried about Grace's future too. Why would I even need God anymore?

In silent screams, with gritted teeth, I said, *"You owe me something!"*

The door to Malak's room slammed shut. It had done this before, I admit, but this had such force that my hair blew away from my face, even though I was five feet away. I challenged God, through clenched jaw and all, "That's not good enough,"

I felt Him in the room. It was as if He answered me: *Be very careful, child of Mine. Be very careful. You couldn't handle it. You have no idea what you are asking.*

As if the true presence of God would require protection under that kind of awesomeness. That if God were to speak audibly, the house would tremble. Or that His gentlest whisper could spawn a tornado, just by virtue of His majesty. His wrath might empty the sea. That the attributes of Him I did not understand could be dangerous, when I know *not* who He is in all His perfection and glory.

That was my first experience with that kind of thinking. This had to be real ...

Because life is very empty. Without Me, can you even imagine your soul's condition of meaninglessness? What of the horrific outcome of all of your lives, when left to your own demise? Really? After this blatant demonstration of your human error, you're that cocky? Watch yourself, child. I do have wrath, and trust Me, you haven't seen it.

I had to admit, it was true. Hm-m-m. I felt humble, as if God had saved me from so many things I never had considered. Every minute of every day. Self-pity could drive me to reckless, selfish behavior, but what would I gain? At what cost to Grace, the only child I had left? Could Grace be at risk for alcoholism and low self-worth or coping skills that were modeled by fragmented parents who would teach her to cave into the face of tragedy? If I didn't owe God anything, I owed Grace more than a shell of a person. I owed Gracie that much.

And then it struck me: If this was life *with* God, what was life like *without* Him? If life was meaningless now, my singular hope to restore it was a miracle or two.

I considered keeping God, just for that day. We would repeat these conversations for a few months. The question came down to "Do you trust Me?" After all the tantrums, the deadening pain, and the tearing of my soul. I had to learn to trust Him again.

I admit I watched hours of Christian television. I floundered. I wondered if I was falling into a cult. Who watches the church channels all day? I believe in living in balance. Maybe I was off kilter? But it was a positive escape. TV wouldn't lash out in anger toward me, leave me isolated, judge me, or hurt me. The preaching of the Word infused me with hope, which translated to peace. Restoring my faith was number one on my agenda, and faith is the very substance of things hoped for, the evidence of things not seen. If there was no future for me, the thing that might work was a real God. The more Christian TV I watched, the more the Scriptures spoke to me and the more my faith grew again. Religion was useless, but a living God might be powerful.

I tried to stay busy. One morning, I hit the treadmill for my usual run. My chest tightened, followed by nausea and labored breathing. Within minutes, I was running blindly across the gym to get to the locker room. Another panic attack. I walked directly into the toilet stall, burying my face so I would not be recognized. I curled up on the floor in a corner, covered my eyes, and cried silently, hoping not to embarrass myself. How humiliating.

At the mall, the grocery store, in the shower, or at the movie theater, I felt cold all the time—snow-shivering chilly in ninety degrees. My stomach was always tight. My knees buckled for no apparent reason. Nausea continued. Like a routine, I wiped the cold sweat from my forehead, got a drink, smiled with happy thoughts, and pretended. Did it again the next day. I didn't want to make it another month, feeling so much pain, much less for insurmountable years, climbing to whatever normal looked like. So as the days passed I made a plan.

First, I would pray. Every day. In between the job interviews and applications, the grocery store and the pharmacy, dinner and getting the mail, I promised myself I would pray about anything and everything, all the minutiae that was bothering me, over and over again, if necessary, until I felt better. There was no amount of prayer that would ever be enough.

Second, I made a list of affirmations and Scriptures, all positive, that I committed to speak out loud over my life every morning, if necessary. I chose to fill my mind with nothing but positive thinking. I made time to read the Bible and study for at least an hour every day while I was unemployed.

I would play Christian music, choosing to praise God in my situation. (Maybe I could have an impact on the mood in the house.) I enrolled in a Bible study finding friends to encourage and pray with me.

But then I would see something of Malak's on the floor, his drawings of the "lemmens" (lemons) hanging on the bathroom wall, or the picture of the grumpy spider with glasses, and I would have to close my eyes.

A running commentary played in my head: *Don't forget to pay the bills. Call the insurance company. Take a phone call. Roll and cry on the floor. Watch Christian television.*

I fell into an empty bed. Chad was in his office—again. I was repeatedly rejected. But give him time. Go to sleep.

When Chad *was* in bed with me, I would watch his sleeping face, and his chin would quiver. I would listen to him whimper. He told me he dreamed of holding Malak every night. No conversations between us. No hugs. No kisses. Only resigned sighs, in "here we go again" style. I would remind him to get the dry cleaning, and he would remind me that Grace had a soccer game.

We went through the motions. Evening parties with friends allowed the dance of life to return like Cinderella at the ball at least for an hour. But when the last guest left, the contemptible stillness returned. It wrapped around my neck like a python. People had worse stories than mine, I mused. *Optimism will get us everywhere, while self-pity will destroy us. I love Chad. I have always loved him. We have had a tremendous, rewarding relationship with its challenges. I felt loved back, in as much as he was capable with his crippled heart. Forge ahead. Drive my life toward a better future. Make Grace's life solid. One day, it won't hurt like this.* My favorite Scripture became, "No eye has seen, no ear has heard, no mind has even conceived what God has planned, made and kept ready for those who love Him who hold Him, in affectionate reverence and (obey Him) and are gratefully called (recognizing the benefits He has bestowed) according to His purpose" (1 Corinthians 2:9).

Grace buffered the pain, but I never realized how empty I had become as a mother. She laughed. Slept fine. Talked easily. At bedtime one night, my small tow-headed baby girl asked, "Mommy, which star is Malak's?"

"Why would you ask me that?"

She went on to tell me that Malak walked on the moonbeams outside her bedroom window at night. He talked to her at length. He told her he missed her and loved her, that he was happy, and he told her not to be scared.

"What else does he say?"

"That I shouldn't be sad. He is happy. He is with me. He likes heaven. He said he would see me again." She smiled.

Speechless and a little jealous, I kissed her cheek and squinted to see any moonbeam at all, any apparition resembling a familiar boy. Resigned and bewildered, I straightened the covers and winked at her. "Good night, sweet baby."

Three months after his funeral, endless questions, an empty chair at the table and countless boring car trips without her best friend was the new normal. But in her sadness, Grace asked me one question for which I was not prepared.

"Mommy?" she hesitated, "when is God giving Malak back?"

I felt the tears fall from my eyes. "Honey, God isn't going to give Malak back."

I don't know who sounded more surprised. Lying down, in such intimate conversation, face-to-face with my precious girl, on the fluffy white pillows of my bed, contrasting her now anguish-cracked face. This was the first time, months later, after funeral, burial, empty room, and all, that she understood the situation?

"He's not? *Really?*" She held her breath like she might explode. Then the outburst of an angry little angel, who now felt cheated by this information. How jaded of me. She had not understood—three months later. I had taken for granted the obviousness of it all, now repugnant in its finality. She hadn't grasped death. She was angry. After waiting for her to breathe, she inhaled a massive amount of air as if she'd forgotten to. Crying ensued.

"Grace, Mommy and Daddy believe in God. When you die, your body doesn't work anymore." I could see she wasn't grasping it. She looked confused. How could I explain it to her? "Malak got an owie in his tummy, and the owie was too big to fix. Sometimes the doctors *can* fix us when we get hurt, and sometimes they can't."

Her eyes radiated disappointment, no longer innocent of the sting of death. "But why didn't God save Malak?"

It was the first question in her seven years that I *could not* answer. I had expected to have every single solution to every single question until she was at least sixteen. It was supposed to be about whether she could have a treat, a cookie, or a friend over. It was supposed to be her wish list for Christmas or an explanation of why her friend was mean. The hardest question might have been, "Why did that boy break my heart?"

"Where *is* Malak?"

"The Bible says that if you believe in Jesus, then you go to heaven."

"What does heaven look like?" she asked, somewhat afraid.

"I think it's got streets of gold, like the Bible says. I mean, I don't know, but that's what I picture. There are no worries about anything, and nothing to be scared of, and no dark whatsoever, not even at bedtime. You don't need sleep. You just have all the safe, happy things in life. Love. Lots of love. Grandmas and grandpas are there, and I think Malak is visiting with them."

"Oh …why can't he come back?"

"I don't think he would want to come back, sweet pea. I think he is waiting for us. We get to see him again, when we die."

"Mommy, I'm afraid. When am I going to die?"

"We … don't know when we are going to die. But God, most likely, will not take you to heaven for a very, very long time. Like when you are an old grandma." I laughed.

"Can you pinky swear, Mama?"

"No. Baby, I can't. But I almost can." I squeezed out a bittersweet smile.

She asked about this many times over the next few years. Every time, my answer was the same. Unfortunately, this was a promise I couldn't make. I had always felt heaven was a place we would see when we were ninety years old. And even now, when life is hard, I just want to quit and go see Malak.

I don't think that I am as afraid as I once was to leave this earth. In fact, I look forward to it. It will be incredible to see what I have been waiting for. Will he be grown up? Will I find comfort? Will I feel pain or remorse many years later?

I was thankful that we had believed in God as a family. Malak understood those concepts. As responsible parents, we had done that duty. I began to understand that if you didn't have a faith in God, you would carry an unrelenting vast expanse of "nothingness" for the rest of your days, with this burden of loss. The living and dying in absolute pointlessness, without God and faith is…sickening, to me at least. Some pursue "knowledge," but for me, there wasn't enough knowledge in the world that would validate the death of a child.

So I began again to choose my faith. Not a naive faith, as thrust upon me from childhood, but a faith that God would find me somehow, too—my God, who had become so real through all this unspeakable pain as a necessary way out. Religion wasn't saving me but a real relationship was, a relationship with Him through my Bible, where God spoke to me through those words on the pages. Not so long ago, these had been empty words. A relationship with God that I had known my whole life but who came and met me halfway in my grief in a more real way. I shut out the world and cracked the Good Book, and wow, was it speaking to me. He was comforting me.

How do people who don't believe in anything bigger than themselves find their comfort? Is it all over one day, and we disappear into nothingness or dirt if there is *no* God? I also realized that heaven wasn't the "selling point" of believing in God—I believed the Bible as His written word—but that I talked to God, and He talked back.

Maybe I won't know why. But I'm learning a lot. I wouldn't trade it.

Ask all the hard questions. Wrestle with God. Ask Him the "why" in your life.

CHAPTER 7

Happy Holidays

I didn't want to shop for gifts that year, but as soon as the Thanksgiving turkey was swallowed, the department store Christmas music began to play. Red ribbons were everywhere. Lit trees with aisles of ornaments and baubles sat prominently next to the clothing and toys. At least Christmas was insanely busy.

Cards, cards, and more cards flooded in. Everyone was so darn cheerful. Their children were all geniuses. They made silly money besides, so "they" bought bigger houses and bigger cars. Even "their" dogs were award-winning pedigrees. The dads were all Olympic athletes. The moms were over-achieving Martha-sweet-tart-Stewarts. All scripted cards competed for the best presentation and color, and the most photogenic, successful, super-star families of the year. Barf. On a good day I might have cared but not that year. I wasn't jealous. Was I? It was just an alternate universe from mine. I admit to being embarrassed by my perspective. *Always be thankful. It will protect you from the whiny, ugly, and dwarfed disposition I loathe.* Nothing is worse than a person who feels the world owes her better than she has gotten. The stench of such a notion motivated me to keep my chin up.

Among the cards was a letter from the county. Curious, I opened it. I never expected what I found so neatly sealed in the envelope. Malak's death certificate, proper and official, a tangible permanence. A pristine, recorded piece of evidence to verify a grotesque truth. A piece of history. I scanned down to the cause of death and closed my eyes. I took a deep breath.

"*Abrasions to the liver, spleen, and femoral artery, ischemic.*"

I scanned for other details and found my hand sliding across the page.

I was both remorseful and reminded of how I much loved him. His age, his parents' names—those little details killed me slowly. I hid the paper away in a drawer for posterity and called my mom, just to feel less alone.

I put off the Christmas gift list as long as possible. Grace had a checkup at a doctor's office. Upon signing in, the doctor's receptionist said, "Checking in Malak?"

"I'm sorry—what did you say?"

"Oh, sorry, Grace, I mean." She laughed.

I offered a small smile and with a lowered voice, I said, as politely as I could, "You can remove him as an active record, please. He is dead."

"Oh, okay. Thank you." She didn't look up.

Afterward, I promptly drove to Kelsey's house to leave Grace for a few hours while I holiday shopped at Target. Kelsey was a funny, sweet neighborhood friend of Grace's; they had grown up together. On one freezing winter day, they had laughed so hard, dressed in snowsuits and half-frozen, that they decided to pee in their pants as a mode of warmth. It was easier. And the giggles were far more fun.

Zipping through the front sliders of the department store, more holiday music added to the bustle, bliss, and vinegar of the whole hoopla. I forcefully pushed past the boys section where cable-knit sweaters and little man-sized blazers hung. A twinge of pinpricks and pleasure. Caught, unwillingly staring, I no longer belong in the world of little boys. I wouldn't get to buy big-boy clothes, a graduation gown, or a tux for his wedding day. My arms swung limp. I dragged my toe to the edge of the carpet and cocked my head. My watery eyes refrained from dripping. Longing to see something familiar, I approached, with caution in my heart. I examined the small cuffs of a blue oxford shirt with button-down collar and flipped through the rack for a size eight. And there it was.

I closed my eyes with my hand on the shoulder. I had to leave. Lifting my head up, I tried to erase the moment. Quickening my pace to the toy section, I surrounded myself with the rows of pink and purple sparkles. I grabbed a princess dress, crown, and large bejeweled earrings and tossed them in the cart. I grabbed as many pink toys as I could find.

Transformers. Darn. He loved them. I threw a couple in the cart, as well as some Legos for the boys on the family list.

Oh my. His stocking, handmade by my grandmother. Should I hang his stocking? Heck, yeah.

I marched over to the candle aisle and picked out a large green one to honor him.

I needed to do Christmas cards. Maybe I would use the last photo we took of all of us on July 4 and make a Christmas card from that. It would be a perfect memorial.

Running into the house, I hid the surprises and dug in the closet for the boxes that preserved photos. What I hadn't expected to see was the box wrapped in purple tissue paper. It was as if it was time to open it. I wrung my hands, staring. Scared to feel. It was months after the accident. I mustered up the courage to unwrap it. Inside, was an envelope with locks of his blond hair, a grief class schedule, a book on explaining dying for Grace, and the most exquisite blue finger-paint handprints. Powerful. Stopping to strengthen my knees, I gingerly put the lid back on my priceless present and opened a box of photos.

There it was! Malak's head and mine were cocked. Malak had an almost reflective smile, serene, not his typical toothy grin. He looked angelic. It was as if the photo had celestial haze over it. Chad and I drafted the Christmas card letter as we prepared to say good-bye to the year and to look forward to a new one to come.

> *Dear friends and family,*
>
> *It is almost impossible to balance this letter between both gratitude for your unspeakable love for us and our broken hearts. For those of you I have not been able to speak to, I apologize.*
>
> *Malak died August 7, 2002, at eight years of age, in a car accident. (He was wearing his seatbelt, and I was driving.) We chose to send the most current picture from the Fourth of July. The details are long and difficult, but Grace is just beautiful, and I am remarkably well. Chad is missing the sparkle in his eyes, but he's hanging in there. He is still working in sales, while I have been off since last April.*
>
> *We wish you all the most that life offers this Christmas. We appreciate your prayers so much. Thank you for all the cards, money, and gifts. It has been amazing. We have a new perspective, if you'll generously indulge me:*

I am grateful to cherish the details of life, like the framing of love notes from little hands and the sweet scent of a cheek and hair. And while bedtime talking can often be an annoyance, it is indeed more priceless than even Visa suggests. The secret to life is no regrets.

Above all, I think it would be remiss for us to not celebrate our faith. Neither of us could imagine a single day without it. God's grace to anyone who would suffer such loss without having at least one *source of hope. If Malak's death counts for anything, let it be that you love deeply beyond measure this Christmas, and consider your own faith and tell your children. Here's to your friendship, your joy, your faith, and success but particularly your life. You matter to us.*

Love,
Chad, Grace, Malak and me

"How are you, honey?" I asked Chad. He and I were resting on the sofa after having put Grace to bed.

"Fine," he said curtly. "You know I don't wanna talk about it."

"I know, but if you can't talk to me ... you have to talk to someone. ... I just want to know if you're doing all right. I love you so much. Just tell me something. Anything."

Breaking the silence, he said, "I was thinking maybe you should take some defensive-driver classes, like I had for my work training."

Pause.

"O-kay," I replied. Not angry. Not judging it. Just ... pondering. "I could do that ... if you think that's a good plan?"

"Think about it." He walked away.

This was typical of our conversations. He worked nonstop. The neighbors were concerned we were becoming "shut-ins." We went to a couple of holiday parties. I saw Chad turning inward, but I didn't take it personally. He processed things on his own. I had grown tired of his absence. One day, I picked up the phone.

"Hi, can I talk to you about Chad?"

"Sure, honey. How is my son doing?" Instinctively, Chad's mom knew.

"Ah ... I'm worried. He never talks. He gets mad when I ask anything, especially if I ask how he is doing. I've stopped asking. He's not in a bad mood, really, but he's not himself. He's shutting me out—everyone. I have asked some of his physician friends to talk to him. They say he doesn't ever call them back, except to say it's crazy busy and that he will call later. What do you think? Is there anything I can do? Should I just let him work this out?"

"Well, we grieve in our own way, sweetie. He'll come around. He's strong. He'll be fine. Just keep loving him."

"I think so too. Thanks, Mom. I love you so much. If you have any insight, please tell me." She understood things about her son that I never could get clarity on, until she explained it to me. I would just relax and let things happen. He'd be fine.

"Hon?" she added. "Have you ever considered taking defensive-driving lessons? Maybe that would be good."

"Oh, yeah. Chad mentioned that; I'm not opposed to it ... I guess. Accidents happen to everyone and—"

"You could think about it," she said.

"Yep. Yep. I will. Love you. Thanks for helping me with that. Talk to you later."

"I love you, too. Merry Christmas. Take care, hon."

Maybe I was a little hurt.

I can't earn forgiveness. Or love. I can't make someone love me. And I won't beg someone to. I cannot make God love me more tomorrow. Or earn His love the next day. He already does love me. To grasp a self-love based on who God says that I am, equally embracing all that I am not.

CHAPTER 8

Resurrection Sunday

Spring arrived, but things didn't improve. Chad was more closed off. I had stopped trying to make him open up. It was infuriating and isolating, and his constant rejections attacked my self-worth. You cannot make someone take action. I saw a counselor. Chad did not. He continued to drink. I continued to pray. We didn't have the relationship we once had, but I still loved him and was loyal to him.

The most unexplained miraculous event took place during our vacation in Wisconsin. We were visiting Ty and Sutton and their children for the first Easter after Malak's passing. We planned to rise around 4:30 a.m. for Easter service, but we awoke around 2:00 a.m. to Grace's shouts.

"Mom. *Mom*! I just saw Malak standing over me in my sleeping bag. He was like a ghost but with tiny dots of different colored lights! I closed my eyes because I thought I was dreaming, but when I opened them, he was *still* there! I'm scared!"

Chad pulled her into the bed with us.

"Did he say anything?" I asked, incredulous. "What did he do?"

"He was just smiling."

Chad added, "That's weird, 'cause I saw him too, and he was just now sitting at the end of this bed on my side, smiling at me! I closed my eyes, thinking I was dreaming, but he was still there, too!"

I asked what he looked like. Chad described the same multicolored dots of light.

For a while, we all lay in bed, hoping to see him, to relive the experience. But we had to get ready to attend the sunrise service. If only sheer willpower could make it happen. Odd. On Resurrection Sunday, my son appeared to Chad and Grace. Peculiar that I didn't see him. Was he leaving for heaven forever?

When we returned home, we were once again inside the dark cloud we had run from.

I stopped asking Chad, "How are you?" His clever wit had formed credos like, "Don't ask, don't tell," laughing as he said it. Most people obliged him. I tried the tearful approach. "I'm scared. … I think you need help. You're not dealing with this." No response. Overall, I believed in us. He showed tiny signs of improvement now and then, like a smile and a hug, but an hour later, he was stone cold. So I tried to be patient.

His absences from the dinner table had been a habit all our married life but grew to become the norm. He was not home for dinner at all. I didn't cook for that reason, unless we had guests. Wednesday night hockey, and Thursday night happy hour with the boys. Monday night meetings, and Tuesday night he locked himself in his office, working 'til 1:00 a.m. Eventually, I had a conniption, which yielded—yet again—no change.

Over a year after the accident, Malak's room looked the same (despite promises to myself otherwise). I'd let it become a mausoleum. Because Chad wasn't ready. Chad preferred to talk of Malak in the present tense, I guess to keep him "alive" in some way. His depression was obvious, the signs of choler hidden inside of him.

One weekend, Chad was helping some neighbors who needed a shower installed, a roof mended, and cement poured. He cleaned a friend's three-car garage, ridding it of the three dogs' feces, all day on Saturday—by himself. What a foul job that must have been. He was anywhere in the world but home. His hunting increased, his projects multiplied, along with new single friends. Two things were constant: Belvedere vodka and the silent treatment.

No one could run away from another person so vehemently, unless he *hated* her. Had I become an object of resentment and a target for meanness, exacerbated by alcohol? I accepted it, on the one hand, because it fed my own need for punishment. Likely, he recognized his own self-destruction but didn't know how to kill the gargoyle. Maybe he was afraid; if he opened the floodgates on his anger, what could be demolished in its wake? Part of me was developing deeper angst. He had been absent all these years at dinner and on weekends. Now, he should be a man and get it right. *Be here.*

Handsome and charming in public, he admitted to numbness and described it as having "no shut-off valve." There was a new recklessness in him. When it came to grief, the blind not only couldn't lead the blind, but we had stopped walking next to each other. More like the deaf, mute, and blind.

I didn't understand Chad. *He* didn't kill Malak. What? *I* never intended to kill Malak. What was *he* angry about? Angry that Malak died, sure, but he shouldn't take it out on me.

One late evening, Chad was staring out the master bedroom window. "Babe," he said quietly, "if I can't have Malak back, I don't want the family at all."

I was stunned. Ouch. But it simply illustrated the level of his pain to me.

"I think it will get better, honey. I love you. It's killing me too."

I couldn't look too closely at his resentment; I knew how much he loved me. I didn't know how to handle this conversation, since the repercussions were condemning for me.

I knew that I should examine my guilt with some honesty. A scary proposition with an unforgivable, lasting consequence. If convicted, what would the terms of my prison sentence be? I went into the spacious master bath to my own sink, looking into it. Then, looking into the mirror, I scoured my face as if I hadn't seen it the same way before. I turned on the water to wash my hands. I saw them calmly rinsing under the water but soaked with spilled blood, richly red, freshly thick, and numbingly cold. Absolutely undiluted, even while the faucet forced the cold water. Insoluble. Would that it could wash away clean, but it would not. My own mind games were grabbing at regret and gasping for grace simultaneously. *Reconcile this, if you can.* I truly had done this—like a demented murderer who had not stopped to explore her own part in the killing or like the serial killer who madly claims her innocence. Were there only six degrees of dissonance between them and me?

Chad had built a fake world. Maybe I had, too. He had a wall around his heart for his own happy place—no death, no anger, no pain. No wife. No Gracie. A world where an empty child's bed and little Matchbox cars could not haunt him. Where for just one single day, or even one single pass, we might reach the top of the stairs and not see an empty room. *Chad convinced us that all was well.* Ironically, I had loved him for exactly that vulnerability, had he only let me wrap myself around him. He confided in no one. I had seen him lie outright to his family on the phone for the first time. His guy friends begged to help him, but something kept him too proud to trust that love in many forms would accept all his offerings without judgment. I couldn't save him. I prayed fervently. How I wanted to save him. I believed one day, in his own time, he would get help. If I had just loved him *enough*, he would have felt it inside somewhere. *If* I loved him *enough*. I could see the dark fingers of something knocking on the door of his heart, where something else was inviting him to the party of his life. The dark side, winning. I was balancing that with the accusation that I had killed our son. Family had said as much. Undeniably, I had.

My daughter fluttered her eyelashes before sheepishly posing a question I could tell bothered her. "Mommy, did you kill Malak?"

I saw her face trying to feel safe with me. Did she think I would kill her, too? I had, after all, asked myself the same question many times. I told her that I didn't have a choice to die in Malak's place but that I certainly would have. Accidents happen. I explained that, for some reason, we are here to accomplish something. Fear remained in her eyes. I responded the way any sane parent would.

"I would swim a thousand oceans to find you, to save you, to rescue you from anything. I would die on train tracks, climb any mountain, and search every house. I would rather die than hurt you, most precious baby girl."

Remorsefully, Grace admitted, "Mommy, I took my seat belt *off*. Am I in trouble? I was sleepy, so I laid down." I still marveled that my daughter had lived because she took off her seat belt. Would Malak have lived, if not for the seat belt? *Why was I asked all the questions by the insurance and police about the large and unexplained dent in the back of the middle seat, in front of Malak?* His seatbelt was far too tight to have allowed him to have hit that seat and caused the dent.

I was looking for the horse in the pile of dung. But what good would come from the earnest prayer to trust the "Ruler of all things"? Do I believe in God? Were it not for the golden threads—the door that closed in Malak's room that night or the pennies in Grace's bed that funeral morning—I would have given up. Or Easter morning's apparition of Malak. Trust. In the seemingly weak and golden thread, also known as "the still, small voice," almost unheard in the noise of the current chaos. I couldn't crumble. Yet.

Chad's office was locked. Again. Grace went up, knocked on the door, and crawled onto his lap. Progress. I heard the door open from the downstairs kitchen, her soft footsteps in a "one-two, one-two" rhythm, still nervous on the stairs. She whimpered as if she had lost something.

Pulling on my shirt, she said, "Mommy, something's wrong with Daddy. He's scaring me. He is talking funny," she said.

"What makes you say that?"

"Daddy said that he loves me so much. He wanted me to always know that, if for some reason he wasn't here. Do you think he would hurt himself?" asked my seven-year-old.

I felt a black widow cloak its arms around us. Staring. With goose bumps on my neck and arms, I smiled, lied, and told Grace that Daddy would be fine.

"We need to pray for Daddy." I slid down to the floor, putting Grace on my lap. "Dear Jesus, please protect Chad. Keep him safe. Help. Please. Save us all, from ourselves."

"Aaa-men," Grace added.

Immediately, I called Sutton, seeking a life preserver in a stormy sea. Sutton answered, even at the late hour.

"That's so *weird*," she said. "I was just praying for a hedge of protection around Chad. I had a feeling that something was wrong." Hundreds of miles away, another golden thread.

I waited a couple of days for the right time to address Chad.

In his office, late one night, I pointed my finger at him.

"If you decide to remove yourself from this world, Chad, it's purely selfish of you to do so. There is help, but you refuse. I have been watching you avoid everything for so long that I'm afraid. So please, if you are going to kill yourself, I can't stop you. You have a choice with your life. Please, don't do it in the house, because I would never be able to sell it, and Grace would never recover." Inconceivably cold of me, the powerless, practical, logical side took over. I didn't want to grant him permission. If I was too compassionate, I feared I'd validate his plan. What if I pushed him farther toward suicide? My new job took me out of town every other week. Would I come home to bloodstained walls and carpet in the basement, where he kept his locked guns? How would I protect him? Or Grace? Would I be capable of recovering from his death? I'm not sure.

Picking up the phone, I called Jack, the family nurse practitioner again. "Hi, Jack. I'm sorry to bother you at work, but Chad needs help. He's drinking and avoiding everyone. He was talking to Grace last night as if he wanted to die. I can't tell just anyone, but you are good friends with him, and you might be the rare person to reach him."

"Sure. Let me work on it. He seems fine, but I have been wondering. I'll see if I can get him in."

Chad made an appointment, though he fought me wholeheartedly. I asked to go along so that I could put my perspective on it. If Chad was sincere about getting better, he would want me to join him.

That's not how it went.

"I don't want you there. You don't need to be there. I'm a big boy."

I called his mom, who thankfully rallied for my participation. When we arrived, Chad asked me to stay outside the room while he talked with Jack. Another push away.

Jack waved me inside as Chad exited the patient room. "Chad has every symptom on the depression questionnaire. There's no question that he qualifies for medication, but he's refusing. I'm really discouraged—I can't do anything. This is his decision."

"Thanks. At least I'm not crazy, and *one* person believes me. I can't tell you how huge that is for me. He's keeping it all a secret, and everything just gets worse. I'm scared. Thank you." I smiled at him from the door, ten feet away. I was crisp in my demeanor, so as not to appear weak.

I didn't say anything to Chad in the car. Too tired. Too frustrated.

"We love honestly. You can't do more than that." —My Mom

CHAPTER 9

The Pecan Pie Storm

I admit I could probably torture and kill people with my gift of gab, but it was and is my saving grace. I had talked Chad and everyone else to death, trying to communicate in a way that would break through and fix our life, the catastrophic sinking *Titanic*. It felt like watching someone destruct slowly. My healing became talking. Thinking out loud. Reasoning. The less Chad and I talked, the more I tried, and the worse the tension got, and the further he retreated. I had tried everything. Almost.

It was a black sky, blizzard night. Gargantuan snowflakes made the rural roads elusive. Chad was silent on the entire two-hour drive to his parents' home but became surprisingly good-natured when we got there. I was relieved to feel some semblance of normal. We played Five Hundred Rummy and had a couple of drinks, laughing and reveling in family solidarity and in their incredible home full of good memories and a loving, safe history. The old life (if only pretend) seemed real that day. Relaxed. Happy. For a minute.

"Pass more pecan torte, please. That is so fantastic, Mom," Chad said.

"The salad was so delicious, Mom," I added. "How are Aunt Mary and Cousin Stacy doing?"

"Oh, they are fine, you know. Good, I think."

"Whose bid is it?" Dad asked.

"Jimmy's," Chad said of his brother.

"Did you hear that Tommy got a new house? He needed some help with the plumbing, so I was over there," Dad said. "Wow, what a great little wife he has and just a cute baby. Geez, what nice people. It was fun seeing them." Dad smiled. Always sweet.

"Is that right? I miss them." Chad nodded and grinned back. "You remember the time when we were little, and Jimmy got the cow pie stuck in his ear?" Chad asked. Laughter erupted.

"How did *that* happen?" I asked.

"Jimmy and I were throwing cow pies in the apple orchard when we were kids. I threw one just as he turned his head and hit him in the ear!"

Giggles all around.

"So what happened? What did you do?" I prodded. "This pecan pie is perfect, Mom."

"Well ..." Chad said, looking over at his mom and smirking, "Mom tried to use a vacuum cleaner suction hose to get it out." Again, uproarious laughter, me most of all.

"Really? Did it work?" I pressed on.

"No, we ended up taking him to the family doctor to get it out," Jimmy said.

"Remember, Jimmy, how we hated the dog next door because it yapped all the time?" Chad chuckled.

"You had your hands full with the boys, didn't you, Mom?" I pouted sympathetically.

"Yes, I did," she agreed.

"So what happened with the neighbor's dog?" I asked.

"Well ... ah ... we decided to hoist it up by the collar on a rope just for fun, running through a fork in the tree between the yards. Oh, we could have killed the dog, but we were so little we didn't know. The neighbor came out and was so *mad* that we put the dog down in a hurry."

There was always enjoyment at this house, and this time was no exception. I loved them all. They loved me back.

When it was time to drive home, it was still snowing. Grace was buckled in the rear seat and our black lab, Piper, was in the rear in his cage. With big smiles, laughs, and a thank-you to Chad's parents, who stood in their driveway, our car door slammed shut.

And there it was. Endless, chilling silence all the way home. I began asking him quietly how his workweek was looking. Was his job going okay? Nothing. What was he most stressed about this week? A one-word answer of "status quo." I was not pushy but cautious. I had backed off months ago. He was fooling the world, pretending he was fine, but with me, he was full of blame, and it had become obvious. We passed the accident spot at least three times a month, and every time, the conversations halted. I longed for the day I could do it without tears. I tried to ignore it. The snow was falling in such a thick, heavy pattern, it was mesmerizing yet magnificent. I felt my own rage brewing. Chad did not look at me once in the two hours. Not a grunt or a burp. Two hands on the wheel, staring at the road. His passive-aggressive nature was my punishment. He was letting me know tonight was another penance night.

I felt his invisible hands on my neck like the noose for execution. Though he never uttered the words, I am sure that that night, Chad wished me dead. I understood. I had wished it myself. Never in the eighteen months had he ask me how *I* was. Was I coping? Now, hatred. How I had missed it?

Something in me snapped. I wanted to open my door while driving on the snowy freeway and take my chances. If the car behind me ran me over, fine. I meant it. Twisted, yes. How would I reconcile "killing" my son in my own soul, now or ever? The battles in his heart raged. One side in love with me as the mother of his children. The other side, fury, violent contempt, justified and wrapped in a blanket of his own guilt. It was exhausting, trying to absorb the concepts and events. After a seeming eternity passed in silence, we pulled into our own driveway. I had been holding down my own adrenaline rush. Screw it. I would be heard. Finally. Enough about *him*. Enough patience for *him*. Enough apologizing for *his* mean behavior and of my own enabling.

How dare he wallow in pity? The self-indulgence of falling apart. How selfish of *him*. I had encouraged *him* numerous times to leave, go climb Mount Everest and find himself again. "Take a month off from work, Chad. Do whatever you have to do to get yourself back," I had told him. I had gone to a counselor nearly every week for over a year. He might have lost all of us—what then? He was the one who took Malak hunting thirty feet up in evergreen trees. What if *he* had accidently killed him? I had indulged *him* for all the pining period *he* was allowed. *His* grief and personal space. *His* bitter anger. *His* absences. *His* burning blame. Enough. The truth, however grotesque and honest, had lain dormant until that stormy pecan pie night.

As we pulled into the garage, I was over the edge. I flew out of the front seat and slammed the door. Chad looked stunned, afraid of me, really. I was afraid of me. I opened the back of the Suburban to unpack. With one hand, I let the dog out and threw the very large kennel onto the driveway, sending it sliding five feet on the snow and ice. Grabbing the weighty body-sized bag with one arm, I threw it to the ground with a thud. Grace and Chad stood behind me, mouths open. Things were so tense; no one messed with me there in the garage. My hands shook; my breathing was forceful. I'd held in nearly a year of my feelings about Chad and his grief, the way he tortured me, my own denial and guilt. It was volcanic, yet at the same time empowering. I found a voice.

Chad goaded me, "What the h—? What is the matter with you?"

We exchanged glances, but I said nothing, my face fiery with rage. I felt truly explosive.

I cinched my small bag, took Grace's hand, and went into the house. I set her on the dryer in the laundry room. Grace was shaking and afraid.

"Mommy is okay, sweet pea. I ... need to go for a little drive. I'm mad." *I am out of control, and I can't hide it from her.*

Hearing my trembling voice and having witnessed my outburst, she cried, "You are scaring me, Mommy!"

I put her down. Kissed her. Sent her to her room. She saw my strain for self-control. I went back to the garage, and Chad looked ready for a fight but was a little uncertain of what would come next. I was sure he had never seen me this way.

"What *really* is the matter with you?" he asked again.

"What's the matter with *me*? You—? Oh. I get it. You wanna s-l-o-w-l-y punish me ... torture me. Consider me punished for life! I have already *done* that to myself. What do you *want* from me? Should I shoot myself? Please. Please, let me slit my wrists! You can watch. You can do it, if you like!" I sobbed with gritted teeth. "Should I cut off my arm? Right now, let's do it, Chad! I'll bleed to death, willingly, right here, with your permission. Let's go. *Anything* you want! Cut me into pieces. Bury me in a field. Put me out of my misery. I'd give anything in the world to fix this, but I can't. I *can't*. I would gladly die in his place! I wish this never had happened. What do you want from me? Get off my back! Better yet, shoot me yourself! I *did* this thing! I live with it! I drove the car that killed my son, you—! I gave birth to him. I changed his diapers and fed him. He was my son, too. Stop it. Stop it! Stop! Stop punishing me! You really think *I* wanted *this*? You aren't the *only* one that this happened to. Other people have worse stories than we do. I have gotten our daughter dressed, off to school, helped her with homework, worked my job, cooked dinner, bought groceries, paid bills, mowed the lawn, cleaned the bathrooms, and put her to bed through the entire marriage and especially now, because *you*, Chad, couldn't get it together. Poor baby. The truth is that you haven't been home for dinner more than once a week for years. Now you're never home."

We left each other. A little at a time.

And I had allowed him to become that man. My mistake. I bet he hated me for that, too. I was ruthless and mean spirited. It was bittersweet. There it was. All the verbal swords I had been saving up. It felt like our already fragmented lives, our marriage, our family, and certainly our love were now completely unrecognizable.

I hadn't felt this good in a long time. I got in the car, bought some skinny menthol cigarettes, and just drove for four hours in the storm. Thelma without Louise. Lost. Hoping to want to go home. It was the first time I wondered if I wanted to go home—ever. Other nights, I would get in my car and drive after Grace went to sleep, feeling as though the man in the bed hated me, and I couldn't change it. It became a silly game for me to leave in protest. He had been coming home late for so long. Coming to bed at 3:00 a.m. I continued to feel punished and "hated," and so for all his absences, I decided I had the right to disappear too. He had been running the show without any consequence. What if I had the same desire to run away from it all? If he had those privileges, so did I.

No further conversation. No apologies. Eventually, I stopped entering in the forbidden zone of his home office. I stopped putting up with his absence from my side in the middle of the night. One last time I attempted conversation. Though like Pavlov's dog, going back for a negative stimulus, knowing how bad it would be, I knocked on his office door at 10:30 p.m. He had missed dinner again. Missed Grace altogether. I braced myself. I went in and asked him how his day had gone.

"What the____ do you want?" he cussed and then snapped, "I have a lot of work to do."

To this day, I don't know why I didn't pack my bags without a word that very instant.

Our hatred had bloomed into cold callousness. Gone were the days of "Hi, babe!" with a kiss. I had become a doormat who, in her guilt, allowed his behavior. That was my fault. Guilt had let me let him become horrible.

"What happened to us?" I asked softly, in tears. "You used to pinch my butt. I used to whistle and cat-call when we golfed. We were so ... in love. What did I do?"

He rubbed his face and then his hair, jarring his memory. He squinted his eyes and covered his ears, as if there was no way to ignore what just happened, even though he tried. He was extremely agitated by this question. He swore while contorting his face. "I don't remember any days like that. I don't wanna remember."

There it was. It made perfect sense. *So many months ago, he had tried to tell me*, but I didn't think he meant it. Ouch. Erased without my permission.

I walked out. I had done everything I could.

We teach people how to treat us. Ironically, we can blame the other person for the behavior we allow. We owe the best of ourselves to shine, not our leftovers, when we are with the ones we love. Admittedly, I failed this challenge.

CHAPTER 10

Pinkie Swear

Pink. The color of the thong underwear on my head. Gracie threw her body back on her pillow, giggling.

"How about you put this orange pair on your head," I said. "Come on!"

"Mommy, you're so siwwy."

We laughed some more.

We shared a short sweet smile between us, staring at each other. I pondered how happy I was to laugh and to treasure her here with me.

"I feel like I'm in a box of white walls, no doors, and no windows," Grace said. "Malak left. Daddy left. It's just you and me in the box. I'm glad you are in the box with me, Mommy."

"Is that really how you see it?"

"Uh-huh." She nodded—so adorable.

"What makes you say that?" I asked.

"I don't know. Daddy's not home. It's jus' us's all da time."

"I feel like that too." I kissed her head.

How funny, how true. Chad had left us the day Malak died. I had the same image in my mind, though I never told her, of the two of us in a white box, without food or furniture. Without windows, without doors. No escape. I was equally relieved to have her with me in the box. I, too, felt abandoned.

"Don't leave me, 'kay?" Grace asked in desperation.

"Pinky swear. Eskimo and butterfly kisses. I will never leave you, baby girl. I promise."

The following Saturday, I pushed the mower into its proper place in the garage. My eyes fell on the bag of items hanging from a utility hook. I had actually overlooked it so many times. Today, it stared back at me with intent. One day I'd asked Chad what it was. Its contents were from the accident. My cousin had retrieved items for us from the junkyard where the van was towed. I didn't really know what was inside. The contents couldn't just *be* there for twenty years. Pulling the sack down. I peered inside. Oh. Crap. It was the clothes that had been cut off Malak, with unexplained dried blood. His Game Boy. A children's book that looked like it had been taken from a war zone, bent and tattered. My damaged number-three golf driver, found underneath my seat, flung from the rear of the car. A haunting echo of Malak and Grace giggling and howling. I hung the bag back up.

I wanted to tenderly carry Chad's brokenness with the utmost protection. To mend by embrace, to deflect and fix any sadness in him. Such an extreme contrast to how I used to get so frustrated by the mere lack of milk or bread in the house. What was that simplicity like? Nothing in life is promised to us.

I wish I could tell you that this was the end of this sad story. This is the beginning, truly. The beginning of the hardest part, but the most incredible gifts came through the hands of tribulation. I have heard it said that the kiss of Judas got Christ on the cross to save many. Or that it's not our friends that make us better people but our enemies. It's hardships that shape us.

Drink the happy Kool-Aid.
Dance with underwear on your head.
Dance badly, even, but dance.

CHAPTER 11

Bliss and Vinegar

My biggest problem was gradually taking up residence in my life, yet it went undetected. It was insidious and manipulative and would prove to be fatal to anything left standing in my dilapidated life. I was wrapped in a place of safety and trust and with a vulnerability that I never expected, where surely nothing worse could happen. How mistaken I was about my enemy. With a friendly smile, my enemy knew how to reach my once-safe castle. I opened the door and let it in, confident that I was finding the help and rescue for which I was so desperate.

Already a battle-tired family, we had leaned heavily on all of Chad's coworkers since the funeral for our social outlets. That was an arduous task for our friends but one they did selflessly and willingly. Tuesday night for margaritas, and Fridays for a game of Five Hundred. They supplied us with diversions, an oasis of love, supportive, and patient indulgences on a biweekly basis.

Enter the Johnsons.

Caroline Johnson (Chad's business peer at the finance firm) and I had met only a few times, but we found ourselves spending more time with Caroline and Ryan, mostly because they didn't have a son, which was helpful. We had a blast together, shopping, planning dinners, and parties. Caroline joined my family for the annual women's Christmas shopping day, followed by dinner, dancing, and a hotel stay in the city. We donned swimsuits and lingerie at Victoria's Secret and talked about improving our bra sizes and our rear fenders. She hugged me early one Saturday morning when I arrived at her house for morning coffee.

She smiled gorgeously and said, "You look beautiful!"

"Oh, thank you. Yes. It's tough for two women to be this amazing, brilliant, and breathtaking, isn't it?" I giggled and handed her a wrapped birthday gift. She poured me coffee and placed my favorite vanilla creamer and a Splenda packet on the kitchen island next to my mug. "How's your week been?" I asked. I couldn't wait to hear.

"Good, really good. The girls are doing well. Work is excellent. Ryan bought me red roses, and we went out for dinner last night. He picked out a bracelet. Are you guys coming over tomorrow for dinner?"

"Sure! What can I bring? How about that new appetizer I was telling you about? I'll bring a bottle of cab, too. Now open your present?" I pushed.

"Okay!" She giggled, unwrapping the package. "Oh, thank you. I love these earrings! They're Swarovski crystal earrings, just like yours!"

"I thought that would be fun."

For several months, like anesthesia, these light conversations lessened the pain and pulled me from the black hole. Caroline had worked with Chad for a number of years, so she understood his personality, which made her a compassionate ally and helpful in our grieving process. The Johnsons were a charming family, and they had two precious girls who were so easy for us to love, because we had extra room in our hearts already. Famous in my mind for guacamole (Ryan's recipe) and sure-fire fun we enjoyed life when we were with them. As couples, it was rare for both spouses to like each half of the couple.

When we were first married, Chad and I cooked together a lot, but as time wore on, he wanted me out of the kitchen. I catered to him, as a general rule. I admit to not preparing much, as Chad wasn't home anyway, and the kids preferred hot dogs and chicken fingers. We ate with the Johnson family frequently. Caroline would chop salad in the kitchen with Chad, and I would navigate the children, pour drinks, set the table, and pick up the wine and dessert. Fine with me. Chad was so rarely home, if he wanted to play chef, bring it on. I would take my turn cooking at our house, serving filet mignon and mushrooms with wine sauce, as there were more people to appreciate it. The house would fill with laughter instead of silence. Despite our fighting, things began to seem better with Chad and me, overall.

Once, weeks after her birthday, I asked Caroline about the earrings, having never seen her wear them.

"Do they hurt when you wear them?" I asked cautiously, not wanting to make *her* uncomfortable. Then I conceded, "They *are* clips."

"Um …" She paused and then murmured, "Yeah."

"Oh, I'm sorry." I never asked her about them again.

By the second Christmas after Malak died, I had decided to break with tradition and give Chad a gift, a gun that he had been eyeing. Few things make a hunter happier than a new toy. Life was short. Marriage was hard. This year, I wanted two things. He had taken some "guy trips"—his hunting licenses alone had cost more than some mortgage payments, yet I begrudged him nothing, except his presence at the dinner table. This holiday, I wanted a one-carat diamond to put in my wedding band. I posted an ad on the fridge for the sale day at a local jeweler. I also asked for a vacation to Bermuda, and I would get to choose the friends we went with, which was not typical. Negotiation is part of marriage; there were many things I was less assertive on. I chose the Johnsons as our vacation companions. There would be no snake hunting, no opportunities for Chad to disappear, and no work e-mails allowed. I couldn't wait! We seemed to be connecting again in small increments. I would get to steal him away. Fall in love again. Fix his heart. Make it up to him. The ring was a reminder to me of my personal commitment and reward for the struggle.

"Chad, did you remember the jeweler's sale today? They set the diamond for free."

"No. I forgot. Sorry."

Long silence.

"You forgot?" I was ignored again.

Long silence.

"Oh." Chad added. *Oh? That's it?*

I hung up. Hurt because I'd asked for something, again, without response. I wasn't getting talk time. Encouragement. Love. Support. Maybe I just wanted *something* of value from his heart. I was hurt because I would have given him *anything*. Hurt, too, because I'd never asked him for anything on any holiday or birthday. Was I undeserving of this or *any* request? Of his presence at the dinner table? But a work phone call was important. A work function trumped a movie with Grace and me. I was minimized … again. I had become insignificant … again. Rejected. Again and again.

My father had never once rejected me, and I compared that to the millionth time I felt Chad's rejection. He chose to forget and reject me in the most obvious way.

I made my case for the ring and was deemed unworthy. "Chad, why didn't you buy the ring? Tell me."

"Why now?" he demanded.

"I felt like we needed the renewal. I wanted the reward for making it through the past year."

"I'm just not into it this year," he muttered.

The ring, the money, or the marriage?

I admit I had made all the arguments for justification, which I thought were valid—but irrelevant if he didn't want to give it to me.

Frustrated, I called Caroline, complaining about how Chad was all about *his* toys and *his* vehicles, *his* hunting trips and the guns, ammunition, and gear from the sports store. The Suburban, the commercial trailer, the hunting boat, the kayak, the golf gear, and the trips to Canada, Colorado, and Mexico with the guys every year. The extra rack for the back of the vehicle. The poker weekends away. Belvedere with the boys. I told her about numerous times he'd said no to countless movies, no to a million date nights. No to the dinner table during the twelve years of marriage. No to lingerie and candle surprises. No to a kiss on the cheek. No emotion. No dialogue. No affection. No conversation. No honesty. No, I was not able to change his mind about very many things.

We teach people how to treat us. I would have loved Chad on these terms forever, but his behavior since Malak died shifted everything.

I felt underappreciated. I found out later that Caroline led him to the jeweler the next day, and she helped him pick out my ring. He made a wooden box, carved with the initials "C, G, and M" on it. His whole family was there to witness the presentation. I loved it; in my mind, it meant a new start for us. But the joy of it was poisoned too. Who wants a gift she begged for? I never made him beg for a thing. Money was not an issue for us, and we both knew it. He worked hard, as did I. I paid the credit card statement off every month, which this month showed the cost of the ring. I knew exactly what he spent and paid it with my January bonus. I got something I had always wanted, but it tasted like a sweet substitute. Saccharine.

The hall closet kept reminding me to clean it out. Tons of shoes had piled up at the bottom. I saw Malak's penny loafers. I moved them to his room and put them on his bed. I had to grin, thinking of them. He hated wearing them to church. Months passed. One day, one shoe fell on the floor. I knew it had been there long enough to stay put, but heaven (and I) smiled that day. Oh, how he had disliked the shoes. How a penny had a purpose. Another golden thread was tied to love. Something funny, as if Malak was playing a joke on me. I found it amusing.

After a few short months, March was here, and the long-awaited dream vacation arrived—one week in a top-notch, five-star resort on the beach, with multiple pools, beaches, restaurants, shops, marinas, and activities for the kids. Beach magazines, beverages, happy children, perfect skies, and sunny temperatures, all for the asking. A new yellow bikini swimsuit from Victoria's Secret and a fresh romantic mind-set brought Chad and me together. Chad had had quite a few business trips that spring. The work team always traveled together. They watched out for each other. The spouses at home planned dinners together, making the home life fun too. We were a big family. Caroline was beautiful, with her thick, dark hair and brown-berry skin. Her light blue eyes popped against her tan. She had her new swimsuit. We shopped for them together. She had a winning sense of humor and a cute figure. We had been working out for three months in a fitness class, every day at 5:30 a.m., to get to optimal shape.

I booked her hairdresser. We swapped decorating ideas. She was fast becoming one of my best friends. We had so many incredible friends. What a gift from God at the perfect time. Each family added so much to the group. Caroline seemed to finish my sentences. Both Caroline and Ryan were extremely successful in their jobs and led a coveted life of leisure. The Johnsons' girls, Lilly and Eva, were like sisters to Grace. Grace would get jealous of their real sisterhood, but the joy and glee in their ready-to-love hearts lavished unconditional acceptance on Grace.

Upon arrival in Bermuda with the Johnsons, all three little girls were awestruck—as were the parents. Perma-grins, all around. Chad was so handsome and relaxed. Our ocean-view room was a refreshing contradiction to our shadowy past. We arrived at dinner hour. Walking the marina area, we saw the seaworthy yachts rocking in the warm Atlantic breeze. We decided to eat at a sandwich joint. It just couldn't get any more exciting and blissful than this.

Dinner arrived, and ravenous eating put a hush on the table. Chad extolled his delight with his Reuben sandwich. "This is absolutely terrific.

Does anyone want a bite?" We sat outside on the patio, with a full view of international private yachts—brag-worthy, ostentatious, and keenly named vessels. Surreal.

When there were no takers on Chad's sandwich, he said, "Here, Caroline, try this. It's *so* good." He held the fat sandwich so that the meat wouldn't fall out while reaching way across the table to her. Thousand Island dressing slowly fell from her lips as she took a bite. Gingerly, she wiped her chin, as though it was more than just the best bite she had ever taken. The music from *Ferris Bueller's Day Off* floated through my head. "Ooooh, yeah, chicka-chickaw." That was an impressive bite. Somebody here should light up a cigarette.

The kids needed ketchup and more soda from the waitress. I ate so fast that I felt full immediately. I almost choked. I found myself staring at the center of the table, distracted and in a fog. That night, the four adults played some cards for an hour and then went to bed. Our room was adjacent to the Johnsons. We laughed so hard and were having a blast. Chad and I left the sliding glass door open, so that we could relish the sound of the waves hitting the shore.

I dreamed all night. Chad's hand reaching across the table in slow motion, feeding sandwich nibbles to Caroline. The sighs of their enjoyment repeating like torture. Tossing and turning. *Ridiculous*. They had known each other for years now, and we hung out all the time. I spoke with Caroline twice a day. I must be feeling weird because of everything I'd been through. I had never been a jealous person. Maybe paranoia was a symptom of grief.

The morning sun seeped through the open slider as the sea breeze pushed back the rustling blinds to taste kindness for just one second. Chad went running at 7:30 a.m. and came back with coffee for everyone and milk for the kids' cereal. He brought my favorite—hot chocolate with whipped cream. I kissed him and thanked him and got ready to go work out. In our room, I pulled him aside and shyly told him I had absolutely horrible dreams. I requested that he never, never ever feed Caroline food again. He was surprised and remorseful, apologetic and loving. Problem solved.

Most days started the same way. Caroline had duty with her girls in the morning, and I worked out after Chad got back. We would scurry off to the pool at around 10:00 a.m. The adults had snacks and maybe a drink or two, returning to the room around 3:00 p.m. for cartoons, showers, and cocktails. Incredible. Daily euphoria. Chad was happy, joking, funny, and emotionally accessible to Grace and me. Poolside treats and burgers for lunch; impeccable ambience and cuisine choices for the evening. There was shopping, too. Finally, I felt like I could enjoy my life again, if just for the week, without any reminders. The distraction of not missing our son was strange.

And … a relief.

The next day, we all met poolside.

"I'm running for drinks. What are you going to have, Chad?" Caroline was quick to serve.

"What are you going to have?" Chad asked her.

"A piña colada." Caroline, in her swimsuit and shades, smiled.

"Oh, I guess, I'll have one too," Chad said with a wink, his hands rubbing together.

He had complained about sweet drinks and in twelve years had never ordered a tropical libation.

"Okay. How about you?" Caroline tilted her head toward me.

"Bacardi/diet, tall with a lime, please."

"Honey, how about you?"

"Bacardi Coke, thank you." Ryan's dimples were exposed when he smiled.

We made small talk until Caroline returned.

As she handed Chad his drink, I said, "Check out all those cherries. What? Four, Chad?" I pointed to his drink. "And those fancy colored umbrellas, too."

He laughed. "Yeah, I guess you got the boring drinks."

Four cherries and an umbrella for Caroline too. For a few years now, Caroline and Chad had competed to see who could tie the cherry stem in a knot with their tongue faster. Ryan and I couldn't have cared less. We didn't like cherries. It seemed kind of silly.

The third day was typically like the first two. That evening, Chad and Caroline were on our veranda with a predinner drink. Ryan and Caroline's gorgeous daughter Eva was on Chad's lap. Eva was squishing Chad's face in her hands, and inching her face in front of him, and hanging all over him as he were her uncle. "Chad. Chad. Chad," she would say to get his attention. At three years old, Eva was one of the most striking children I had ever seen. Dark brown ringlet curls and long lashes with matching brown eyes. She could steal the heart of a perfect stranger, that one. Charismatic.

When I arrived on the veranda, I felt funny, as if I had interrupted something. I had never felt like that before, but lately, I had been so ultra-sensitive about every little thing, which was not my personality. Chad acted scattered and flaky at dinner. He got up and left for a half hour. His mood swings had become the norm, so I guess I had gotten used to it. He couldn't sleep. He was down at the casino half the night. He had never done that. He seemed thrilled to be alive in the morning without sleep. He was almost behaving like someone with a drug high. Jittery. Intense. Restless. He was extremely talkative with complete strangers in the middle of dinner and would leave us at the table for twenty minutes. What is *that*? I was getting a little freaked out and felt alone in this discovery. Was I crazy? The Johnsons seemed to notice it too, but no one said anything. We just shrugged. We all knew he was going through something. Was I critical? Was I overreacting? On the morning of our fourth day, he had been talking for two hours to an unknown man in the workout room. *Coping*, I thought. *He's coping. I don't know.*

I watched Chad and Caroline walk ahead of us later that day. She laughed, while he delighted in pointing out things. He had a swagger and a laugh as well. I realized how I hated it when he acted so knowledgeable on so many subjects, a trait I had once loved. He was sharing. Maybe Caroline was oblivious. Maybe she was embarrassed by his interest. Or … maybe she was in pursuit. I became more alert to the nonverbal body language.

A couple of hours later, on the poolside chairs, she seemed too close to him. They had known each other for years. Oh. Their feet just touched, and their elbows. Was that a wink? Why was I watching this?

We took group photos, and I saw it in the photo—his arm around her and not me. They were far too familiar.

"Let's take a pic together!" Caroline waved me over. We were in our swimsuits, embracing tightly, like lifelong best friends. Snapshot. "Oh, get another shot without the sunglasses." Caroline snapped countless photos of Grace and the girls most of the afternoon. Was I stupid? Should I go home? How would I explain this to Grace if I did? What about their children? This was my vacation. What if it all blew up in this utopia? What if I was crazy and making this up? I wasn't about to say anything.

I would talk to Chad.

Bliss and vinegar. It seems an irony that we are often served both tragedy and blessing simultaneously by the universe.

— CHAPTER 12 —

More than Just Cheeseburgers in Paradise

Leaving the pool, drinks in hand, Caroline sang, "*If you like piña coladas, gettin' caught in the rain …*"

Tan and smelling like coconut, I had a massage/scrub with Caroline, while the boys watched the kids. A perfect day. Later, I pulled Chad into the bathroom. I locked the door. Grace was quietly watching cartoons and eating pretzels on the bed. She had swum with Daddy all day. So, so happy. The adjoining door was ajar to the Johnsons' room. Tears began a slow trickle down my cheeks. I stared at the floor at first, but I could feel Chad silently gaze at me, with his arms folded. He was scared. I was scared. I felt drips onto my chest, despite the cold resolve on my face. I couldn't have cared less about anything in the world right then.

My speech was slow and deliberate. Almost an inaudible whisper, as if talking to myself. He had to listen intently to even make sense of my words.

"What?" he whispered.

"Don't say *one* word. *Don't. Say. One. Word.*" I was so quiet. Eerie. "She lights you up like a candle, and I never saw it. How did I *not* see it?"

It seemed like forever before either of us said anything. I never looked at him.

I memorized the fleur-de-lis wallpaper design and the gorgeous mirror frame. For some reason, the carving on the trim fascinated me—the way it was painted to match the room. The irony. So much irony. What was that? I scanned the wallpaper in wonder, as if the walls could actually talk and tell me the mysteries that I was trying to grasp. Like the wicked witch in *Snow White*, asking myself and more, to the mirror and all its secrets, who is the fairest of them all? The hush that I felt was a resignation. The irony was that a mirror reflected dimly what I had not been able to see. *When had I missed it? I am most certain of his affection for her. Where did my husband go? Who were we? Who was I? What happened to my life? Everything in my life?*

I couldn't look at him; I couldn't handle his potential denial or any cursory lines. I sat on the toilet lid. My moment of revelation came, looking in a mirror, as I sat on a pedestal intended to remove personal waste into the abyss of the earth. Irretrievable. My marriage was going down the toilet. I wiped my tears, finally, barely making a sound, never taking my eyes off the mirror. I would keep the secret with Chad, since I assumed that the Johnsons knew nothing. I had discovered the naked truth. Chad kneeled down in front of me, arms relaxed, with his hand in my hair. In all sincerity and trembling, he said, "I love you so much."

I said, louder now, with stern, sure authority, "I know you *do*," with a nod, but I still couldn't look at him. Funny, I recall how certain I am to this day that the man loved me. He said he wanted *me*, as I walked out of the door in slow resolution.

"Where …?" he began.

"I'll be back when I'm ready."

The charade. I went downstairs in a daze to purchase the skinny cigarettes, like a drug addict shaking, trying to light up. I hid near an ashtray by a rear hotel exit, crying and staring into space. I noticed a woman reading my face. She had been there. She knew something horrible was happening to me. The joke was on me in a game I didn't want to play. A half hour passed. I had to return to the room. Chad was jumpy, wondering what I would do next. I showered. He asked nothing. I said nothing. Ready for dinner, we checked the girls into a play-camp. I only had adult eyes to fool.

"Is everything copacetic?" Caroline asked.

Am I pathetic? I was stunned by her question. *Why did she ask? Had Chad texted her that they had been discovered?*

"What's going on?" she asked, tilted head, compassion in her eyes, pout on her lips.

What if she *was* doing this? This would make for interesting actress/detective work. Screw her if she was guilty. I would nail her to the cross myself.

All evening, I watched them. How much did she laugh or smile? We went to the casino. Drank a little more. I felt dimorphic, insecure.

We had gone deep-sea fishing and eaten the fish we caught at dinner. Yesterday, we'd slid on water slides, and watched our children with simple, divine pleasure, and shared the most personal of laughter. I could only assume that my best friend could not do this to me or to a man who had lost his son, when she knew he was compromised as a person. What about her husband and children? I promised myself to forget about it until I got home from vacation. Just a couple more days. Anything else would be a sad waste of a lot of money on my first and potentially last vacation. But I believed I would get Chad away from Caroline when I got home, and things would work their way back to normal—maybe. Who knows if or what their relationship really was? I couldn't tell. He clearly was into Caroline.

The next day, Friday, we decided to go on a moped island tour. I was hesitant, but I wasn't about to be the dark cloud now. I already felt like a tagalong on Chad's date. This was our last day. That I was relieved was an understatement. Who would have guessed I would beg for deliverance from my own handpicked dream vacation?

If there was a more breath-stealing oasis diverting me from my reality, I have never found it. Interestingly, it was the Last Supper. The last hurrah. The last of many things, including my view on my best friend, my marriage, and my future. My family. My home life. My loss of confidence. My naiveté. My sexiness. My sacredness. My core consistency. We toured the island for the afternoon. Emotions ran in my head that day, holding onto Chad around his waist, as we shared a moped. He stopped to take pictures of a sculpture with a mother and child. "I'm gonna make one like this for you," he declared boldly.

What was that? Lovely. No wonder I was confused.

Nearing the end of the ride, rounding the last bend, the moped slid in the sandy gravel on the curve in the road. We tipped, slipping sideways on the pavement. I felt my elbow drag and scrape the gravel into my skin. My head spun, thinking about whether we would hit oncoming traffic in the road. I was back in the car with Malak and Grace, with racing snapshots, everything in slow speed. Who might die? When would we stop? Was Chad injured? I realized that Ryan and Caroline were skidding so as not to hit us. I felt a tire run over my left hand. My right hand, once squished under the moped, was now free. But the fake diamond ring I wore for travel was pinching on that hand. I felt dizzy. Sleepy. My right hand ring was pinching. My right elbow hurt.

Someone was kind enough to call the ambulance. "No, she'll be okay," Chad said in an easy tone.

It was Caroline that I heard whispering, "Chad, you have to call for help! Look at her elbow." He didn't care about me. He just wanted to go play.

I passed out, maybe only a few minutes. In an ambulance, the EMT attempted to cut my ring off my swelling finger.

"Ouch! M-m-m! Ouch!" I said, a little hazy.

"I'm trying to save your diamonds," the EMT said.

"Oh! Just cut it off!" I laughed, relieved. "It's a thirty-dollar ring from Target. Go for it!"

"Really?" She laughed along with me. Everything in my life seemed as fake and as smashed as that ring.

Caroline and Ryan returned to the hotel and got the kids from camp. I was treated with morphine and a scrubbing of the slice in my arm, measuring three inches in length. I remember laughing and feeling good for the first time since before Malak died. Drugs. No wonder people got addicted to morphine. The seduction of pure, unadulterated peace. Engraved in my mind, however, was the road rash that Chad had from both of his shoulders to both hands and down one leg. Blood. Gravel enmeshed in his skin. He had buffered the fall for me. I didn't have road rash. Chad refused the use of any drugs at all. I looked at him in dazed disbelief. His face, bizarre, numb, and not a peep came out of him. I think they gave him something to bite on for the pain. They scrubbed his skin bloody. I have never seen anything like it. It made me think he must have been on something to handle it all. I couldn't watch; it made me nauseated. Even the physician shook his head. It was the first time I wondered what possessed him to endure this. I may never know the real reason. Was it that he wanted to feel something? Anything? Torment or pleasure? Numb too long from Malak's death. His mind must have been flying. Crazy emotions. *A forbidden love affair in wild, hot pursuit.* Maybe he felt punished? Guilty. Self-destructive in paradise. Severe depression brought on by the insurmountable grief and horrendous, untreated anger long unprocessed. His animosity now manifested in punishing ways. I was incredibly blind to it all, but I can now see it as if through a microscope.

I was lost in my own experiences, crawling up from a hole that went to the center of the earth. His isolation was masking much of his internal inferno. My antagonism helped justify his isolation. How convenient. A field of hidden "minds" full of deceptive plans and sick emotions. My reality shifted. Surprises lurked in the dark. What would these minds conjure up?

I was willing to wear the blame, easing my guilt. I still carry the five-thousand-pound bag of responsibility on my back for getting him into this mess.

Grace suffered from anxiety attacks after the accident, fearful of losing a parent or of separation in general. Chad was wrapped in bandages around his chest, down one leg, and around both arms. I had two wrapped arms, a crooked pinkie finger on the right hand, and a small fracture in the left hand. The elbow might require surgery; the flesh torn down to the bone. The ER doctor in the Bermuda hospital recommended waiting until we returned home to have surgery performed, in case of infection.

When we returned to the hotel, Caroline agreed to wash my hair, since neither of us could get our bandages wet. My husband was in love with my best friend? Abasement. I'd rather be anywhere in the world but in her hands. I was dependent on my enemy and my betrayer. I was amused by how much sand came out in the washing, like the truth rinsing out and revealing the hidden secrets of my life. After a silence, I said with mixed feelings, "I know this is terrible to say, but maybe now Chad can understand how thirty seconds can change your life. No one is immune from an accident."

She was quiet. The look on her face disapproved of my comment. Perhaps she was wondering if I understood all that Chad had been through; she was Chad-sympathetic and undeterred from the task.

Yet another irony, we had intended to fly home together, but when booking return flights online, the seats were full, so I booked our family on a separate return flight from the Johnsons. God knew what I did not. Thank heaven.

Chad and I didn't really speak, starting with the cab ride to the airport. Through security to the gate, Chad's blood was seeping through his many bandages, and I looked equally conspicuous. Like mummies walking, according to Grace. We both found that the swelling was uncomfortable, so we elevated our arms above our heads, passing gate by gate, and on the seat in front of us on the plane ride. Everyone stared. They felt so bad for "those" poor vacationers. They couldn't even begin to guess the unseen hemorrhaging. They probably saw a nice Barbie-and-Ken suburban couple who'd had a bad accident. But underneath my skin, everything was bleeding profusely. They certainly couldn't imagine the death of a son, scraped-up hearts, or my deteriorating marriage.

I kept seeing their compassion. The paradox was that I wanted to stand on a chair in semi-hysterics and shout out my afflictions. *This is nothing! My life is a medical bleed-out, and I can't do anything about it! I am not equipped to fix it! I wanted someone to save us!* Would—could—*anyone* rescue us? I wondered, too, about my daughter and the effects of all of this on her future. The grand unraveling was far more caustic than what she could ever see. The once picture-perfect story had slipped into a trashy novel. It was as if, by mistake, a door had been opened on the day Malak died. From a family creed to erased lives.

I would keep my enemy close. To catch one thief and one liar, I kept things under the microscope. Thankfully, this would be the end of it. Chad and I had been together for many good years. Caroline was an arrogant girl if she thought she could undo that in one month. It couldn't have been going on longer than that, right?

Forgiveness will set you free, not the one you spend your blame on. When I'm not sure "who" I am, I should remind myself of "whose" I am.

CHAPTER 13

The Breakdown

No sooner had the bags been brought into the house than Chad handed me the phone.

"Would you like to come over for dinner?" Caroline asked.

Awkward! Is this the start of the poker game? We were obviously playing big-stakes craps. Chad appeared afraid to RSVP.

"I don't think so." I assumed she knew why.

"Why not?"

Here we go. I'll kill her. I avoided conflict. I knew this about myself. But once you cock the trigger back—and I was holding the gun—you better step aside for the bullet aimed between your eyes. It's not like she didn't know this day would come. She's calling the game? Bold. Stupid. Crazy b—. Yet I was compelled to bluff. Let's see what she will do. She had balls. Chad was still quiet as a mouse. He never left the room.

Imagining that my best friend could do this was really hard to wrap my brain around. Pretending not to know prevented obscene screaming on my part. If I acknowledged this, I might go "cray-cray." I pride myself on sane behavior. I didn't know how I would behave. Ignorance required no confrontation until I was ready to speak to her. The right answer would have been, "I don't wish to speak with you." Or just hang up. Unfortunately, I couldn't think straight. Feeling a bit like Kathy Bates in the movie *Misery*, merciless. Maybe, I did myself a disservice. *Do I always have to be the sane one?* I was tired of being well-behaved—dependably mild and sweet. I contemplated which direction to take this conversation.

I was thinking at warp speed. *Choke and slap her. Go ahead. Barbaric, yes. Pull her hair. Embarrass her—that would be satisfying. Wait. Why beat her bloody over my disloyal husband? He was the one who betrayed me first. He was my issue. I'd love to blame her, but …*

Or maybe self-control was the higher standard of valor and classy behavior. Is that spineless? I can't say.

Did she know everything? If I asked, they would both deny everything. Or was she unaware of his fascination? No. She's the one calling here, so … that's brazen of her. She's pushing now.

"Ryan thinks there's something going on with Chad and me. How do you see it?" Brilliant phrasing. No denial. No admission. I had expected more integrity from her. Silly me. Integrity left when the clothes came off. Why the dinner invite? This was really screwed up.

I shot off my mouth, but as mad as I was, this was my close friend. I felt guilty, furious, insecure, and dirty. Nonsensical, duped, and disrespected. *I see it, all right.* That was a calculated, perfectly constructed question, designed to allow her some control in directing the conversation, in her favor. Manipulation, one of her talents. The most successful sales training programs had served her well.

"I concur." I didn't know what to do next. "Haven't we seen plenty of each other for a week?" I asked tartly. "Are you kidding me?"

"I'll come over right now!" she pleaded. "Nothing happened. Just let me come over!"

Lie number two hundred. How do I know the truth? If she comes over, they will placate me, belittle and insult me, and I'll be explosive and then repentant for my anger. She can't come over. Why can't I verbally abuse her? I didn't know.

"No." I hung up, overwhelmed. Caroline was opening Pandora's box, especially since Chad hadn't said one thing yet. She had attended the funeral, held my hand, hugged my child, and served me dinner. She had kissed my cheek daily and knew the intimate details of my marriage and, it seemed, every inch of my personal life. She knew my bra size but his shirt size. My insecurities but his dreams. Worst of all, she knew our greatest vulnerabilities. Who was this woman? How did I get here?

We roamed the house in silent corners for a couple of hours.

"Chad, you should quit your job. It's the only way out of this."

"Wait. Then what? We go hungry?" He sounded offended. "I leave tomorrow for another trip." He was going, even if I hated it.

"Will Caroline be on that plane?"

"Yeah."

His job paid some sizable bills, and our finances were the only stable pillar we had left. I had absolutely no idea what to do next. All my shortcomings over the years must have driven him to this. Now, I was too spent to fight. Too scared to hold on. Too angry to speak. Too guilty to have perspective. Bewildered. Weak. Numbness was so welcome, but I couldn't find it. Still bleeding through bandages. Not even unpacked but beaten down.

To be honest, I don't remember that night. I can't recall any of the conversation—maybe there wasn't much. Most embarrassingly of all, I hid in the main floor powder room. Crying and whimpering with paltry pleas for his sympathy. I had a breakdown of sorts, leaning over my knees, pants down around my ankles. Searching God. Despicable. Beggarly. Casts on both arms from my elbow to my fingers. Standing up in the bathroom, maybe to make a final statement, I walked into the living room and fell on the carpet with cascading bellows. Chad's face never looked more disgusted with me.

"What *is* this? Get up. Get up," he insisted.

"I'm … so broken. That's it. I quit. Congratulations. You win. I *hate* you!" Even hearing myself say it was awful. I'm … unfixable.

"You should never tell someone you *hate*," he admonished me. "I would never say that."

"No. You just *act* like it, all day, every day," I blubbered into the carpet.

"We will talk about all this when I get back. We can think better then. I'm going to bed."

That's when I knew I was losing it. That's when I cracked. Ashamed. Weak. Rejected. Poured out to empty. I have never felt as "hated," never as small. A perfect stranger could never devalue me the way the love of my life just had. I must be the worst excuse for a human. What kind of horrible person was I? I *must* have deserved this. I must have loved him immeasurably, because love and hate are close cousins. You can't hate someone you never loved. Help me.

The alarm went off at seven. Chad grabbed his suitcase, glanced at me, and gave a small smile.

"Are you having an affair?" I whispered.

"No," he responded with disgust.

"I love you."

"Yeah. You, too."

Perfectly sculpted circumstances are set up for the forces of darkness to find the pinnacle opportunity to disassemble lives. Denial is a cruel yet desirable animal. I never got to discuss this. He never admitted to an affair. His cold behavior demonstrated either a lack of interest in the matter or meanness, out of guilt. In either case, my husband would be on a trip with a woman he daydreamed about. The company had paid for the tickets, and they had given him tremendous grace over the prior eighteen months. He would focus on his job. Some time to sort my thoughts was needed anyway.

I should have left that day.

With two hands wrapped in casts to the elbow and working as a sales rep, I needed a driver to get me around. Super-duper. I was so thankful for a great job. My driving record had a fatality on it. I certainly couldn't drive the car and risk not having complete command of the steering wheel. Mom became my driver, hair-washer, cook, maid, and counselor—poor thing. What a saint. I told her everything. I wore her out all day with my fifty-two thousand tidbits of utter rubbish, questions, and rants that erupted out of me. But for the first time, I didn't feel alone in the house. It had been a long, long time.

The phone rang.

"Hey, is this an okay time to talk? It's Ryan."

"Yeah, hi, Ryan. I'm so glad you called. Do you think they are having an affair? One of Chad's work partners called to say that they think something is still going on."

"I don't know. I don't hear anything. You keep watch, and I will too. Let's share information. I don't think they are …"

"I'm not so sure, but we'll have to see. Thanks for the call. Hope you are doing okay."

"Yeah. I will check in again if I think something's up."

"I'm glad I have you to swap info with." I smiled to myself.

Ryan laughed. "Me too."

We hung up.

Turned out, Chad won a national award while on his trip for his work achievements, but ironically, he was having his own breakdown, agonizing over his demons and his conscience. He never mentioned it, but I heard about it. I was smoking skinny cigarettes in the garage regularly after Grace went to bed. She busted me one day, bawling. In front of my mom, Grace read me a sermon on the ills of cancer, but her disappointment in me was a real motivator to quit. A wise person once said, "Smoking is simply a root of an insecurity in you. That's why you do it." My mom, who had great disdain for cigarettes, responded to Grace's precocious lecture by saying, "Grace"—she raised her eyebrows—"cut your mom some slack. Let her *be* right now."

"But—" Grace started.

"Grace." A stern voice from Grandma, and Grace stormed off. A smirk found its way onto Mom's face.

I don't think I will ever hear my mom defend smoking again.

"Thanks, Mom. I'm already unhappy with myself. Now, my little daughter can serve me a can o' behind-whoopin'." We started snickering so as not to be overheard.

When Chad returned home, we agreed we would stay together, but I warned him not to let Caroline interfere with our life more than the employment required. He made no admission. I think we swept it under the rug, hoping it would go away. He agreed to distance himself from her. He seemed to be able to work deftly. For the next five weeks, Chad was washing my hair in the sink. Every morning. Intimate. Vulnerable. He felt like a stranger to me. Silly, but I had an irrational fear that he would burn me every time he turned on the water, every single morning.

We'd meet at the kitchen sink. Chad would test the water for temperature and then move the nozzle over my head and proceed. I never told him my fear. Forty-one days later, the day to remove my casts, he tested the water as usual. I sighed in relief, and he moved the nozzle to the back of my neck. Immediately, the fire radiated on my neck with increasing intensity. The temperature shocked me, and I flew back from the faucet five steps, howling. Eyes bulging, I nearly slapped him on impulse. On the last day, he scalded me.

Always trust your gut instincts.

I had red skin for several minutes afterwards. His last opportunity to punish me, and he took it.

"I. I …I'm … s-sorry," he stammered. His face was blank. Not surprised. After that, I noticed something new about him.

"Why aren't you wearing your wedding ring?" I asked.

"You know, the diamond is too gaudy for me. I'd rather have a different one."

"Okay. Go pick one out." I was confused. He had worn that ring for about eleven years without a problem. "Why didn't you tell me?"

"I don't know. It's not my style, really."

Not good. There must be a different reason. He looked so sincere when he said it.

I kept in touch with Caroline as before, and over time, we ate a dinner a week together. Mostly to keep my enemy close. Everything seemed under control. For my birthday, Chad got my favorite shrimp recipe from a restaurant I love. He surprised me with a fabulous dinner, wine, and a babysitter for Grace.

A week later, as I was looking out the front window, Caroline stopped by to deliver something to the house. She and Chad were talking at the edge of the driveway.

I watched. I opened the front door. They saw me and looked awkwardly at each other after they noticed me.

"Don't act like you don't know each other," I called out, condescension in my tone.

"How was your birthday?" Caroline asked, walking up the front steps, bearing a gift of a bracelet.

"Fantastic." She drained me with her presence and her pointed question. "What did you do?"

Now I wondered if she already knew. "He made me my favorite dinner."

"And how was the … you know?" She smiled.

Why did she just ask me that? "Oh, he's always stellar in that department!" I assured her. *Wow.*

Neither of them admitted to any affair. I supposed that they would have cooled off for obvious reasons since they had been caught—sort of.

"Ryan, It's me," I said into the phone. "Can we meet?"

"Yeah. I've been wanting to talk to you, too." He conceded.

"Okay, good. The same parking lot, lunchtime. Say, Subway sandwiches?"

"Perfect."

I got into Ryan's car, and we hugged. Unwrapped sandwiches.

"It's so great, conspiring to catch them," I said after we exchanged pleasantries. "It feels … safer. Empowering, somehow."

"I know. I feel that way too," he nodded. His face brightened. "You look so nice today!"

"Thank you. I appreciate that. Is that a new shirt?" I looked closer.

"Yes, do you like it?"

"Very nice. Put some pep in your step. Looking good, Mr. Johnson." It was quiet a moment. "Sometimes, Ryan, I think they are so having an affair, because what he does and says makes no sense. He's mean. He's never home. I heard that he had some sort of breakdown on the trip. I don't know, because he didn't tell *me* about it. The rumor is he still wants to be with Caroline. What's your perspective?"

"Caroline doesn't talk. She's normal, kinda. But she's working a lot too. I don't know."

I jumped in. "It's been weird with her. She was over the other day, acting like she and Chad wanted to hug but didn't 'cause I happened to be there while they were talking in the driveway. She asked me if I had sex for my birthday. That's totally weird. What the—?"

"I don't know." He sounded disturbed. "Do you usually talk about that?"

"No. Never had a girlfriend who asked."

"Weird. She's been quieter and maybe a little grumpier than normal."

"Is she in her office more, later at night? Home at the usual time? I'm sorry. The whole thing makes me—"

"Yes. Actually, she has been downstairs in the office more. Hm-m-m." He was thinking.

"I question everything now," I said. "I hate that."

"I called her the other day. She took a long time to call me back, and her reason …"

"Chad asked me where I was gonna be traveling for the day and when I would be home last week. He's never really asked me that. I might lie from now on. Be less predictable."

"I came home from work one day and I thought I saw Chad's car leaving the neighborhood, but I decided it couldn't be." Ryan confessed.

We paused and exchanged a look. He sighed. I bit my lip. Even the air was painful.

"We have to get back to work. Keep going!" cheered Ryan.

"Yep. Thanks."

We hugged. Kissed on the cheek.

I got out.

Two months passed. Our anniversary was soon to arrive. Chad and I devolved into perpetual arguing. I threw the phone at his head. I didn't trust him. He had such a social life away from home, and I had become the maid, babysitter, lawn and garden tender, laundress, and bill-payer. Heck. I was just a person on his payroll. Years of absence. Eighteen months of anger, isolation, and suspicion.

"What are you doing tonight?" he asked on a Friday night, putting on his shoes.

"Nothing. You wanna see a movie?"

"Ah. I have. I'm getting together ... with Rich. He's gonna show me his new sports car. Asked me if I wanted to drive it." Symptoms of fast women and fast cars. Classic sideways communication, rather than forthcoming in nature.

"You're not home anymore. You look at me like you hate me. The most excitement I've seen on your face is for driving Rich's car."

"Knock it off. Go and find your own friends."

"You used to be my best friend. You greeted the garbage man like he was Santa Claus this morning—so much kinder than you speak to me. You treat the dog with more affection. You give your entire Saturday to cleaning up dog poop for a friend. Really? What does that say? Everyone else but me. It's always been like this. *Hasn't* it?" I screamed.

It's probably normal to feel trapped sometimes. My screams stemmed from helplessness and futility. I had few friends to call my own but most were his work friends. Had I let everything in my life entwine with his? Now, I resented giving him my trust and my devotion as a wife and the trashy refuse that had come of all that I worked for, valued, created, and loved. Fierce, impetuous yelling went on for an hour, only to return to silence for a few days. I kept expecting him to leave me for her or beg me for another chance, but since neither happened, I assumed he wasn't running to Caroline ... so maybe they were over, if they had started at all.

On our anniversary night, which arrived only a couple of months past my birthday, the tension sucked out any oxygen from this house on fire. Neither of us wanted to celebrate. Both felt unloved and disassociated. We planned to go out for dinner, just the two of us. I don't think we wanted to, but that's what you do. The lovely Caroline had planned her birthday party with mutual friends as a girls' night on the same night. In retrospect, that was a telling choice. Sitting on the couch, considering options, Chad looked up, disinterested. As if his sighs told me what a pain this was going to be, he handed me an anniversary card. I handed it back.

"Chad, you are not in this marriage. If you want out, get out. Don't give me some card that tells me how irresistible I am, how much you love me, or any other crock of crap that's a lie. Don't tell me your ring doesn't fit, or that you never liked it. I don't care. If you've checked out. *Guess what?* I have, too. I can't make you love me, and I am tired of trying. Chad gets whatever Chad wants—toys, free time, women, self-pity, and no commitments whatsoever to Grace or me. Poor Chad doesn't even have to get any *help* if he doesn't *want* to, 'cause *he* doesn't think he needs it. I am taking my ring off. Don't you dare get me some suck-up present and tell me how I mean the world to you. You think about what you want out of this. I'm going out with the girls!" I put my rings in the drawer.

His eyes were big and brown. He sunk sideways into the couch and said nothing. No remorse. No apparent anger. I knew how twisted this was. He must have found it amusing that I was going to be out with his girlfriend on our anniversary.

Caroline was ecstatic all evening. I don't know why I didn't put it together at the time. But it was her birthday, so why wouldn't she be? Suggesting a contest of who could get their mouth around the Irish cream/whipped cream shot without using her hands, Caroline won. She texted all evening. I noticed a bit more whispering side chatter among the other girls. Caroline quietly told me, when no one was listening, that the jeweler, when they had gone to get the ring for me, assumed the ring was for Caroline. Add insult to injury. Nervous laughter. Why would she tell me that? To humiliate me, that's why. Her competitive side was showing. It was the one present that every wife dreams of getting from an adoring husband, but now I had all this mental garbage attached to it—minus the most important part: the lovesick, loyal husband.

The girls all looked so sorry for me. I ordered another Bacardi/diet with a lime. I didn't care. The gossip was about to begin. Caroline and the other girls. The "other girls" knew about Caroline. It was all sick.

It was the only dance joint in town. His name was Rico. Suave. Gorgeous brown eyes stared at me across the room and made their way close enough that I could see the flecks of gold in them. Spiked-in-the-front hair. Killer jawline. I look him up and down. Hot baseball player uniform, looking like trouble.

"Do you want to dance?" His dimples begged me.

I hesitated, seeing his lips, and tried not to lean any closer.

"Yeah." I smiled.

He slid his fingers between mine and led me to the floor. Dark tan. Muscles. He looked me up and down subtly, and shook his head like my last name was Klum. Raising his eyebrows, he lifted those thick lashes on the puppy eyes, as if to ask permission to put his hand on my back. Slowly, he pulled me in closer. *Kill me now. I feel ridiculously, intoxicatingly beautiful.* Wow. He didn't see anyone else in the room. What a contrast. I'd never thrown myself at a man. Or begged to be loved. No pouting tonight. Just a few harmless dances. A couple hours later, my friends all had left. The bar closed.

He took my hand and walked me outside and around a quiet corner. He pressed me against the brick wall, just outside the club, and sealed the night with a kiss. Are ... you ... kidding me? I'm sorry. It *is* what it is. Broken on the inside makes broken on the outside.

I went to his house. Too drunk to walk the stairs, but I made it. After only a few minutes, feeling remorse crawl into my brain, I told the unsuspecting guy my situation, apologized, and told him I was going home, though I wished I could stay. He nodded and told me that my friend Caroline had encouraged him to show me a good time, because I was going through something. I kept my clothes on and most of my dignity.

"Wow. That's funny. She's the girl who is *having an affair* with my husband."

"Whoa. That's. A little ... sick."

"Yup." I drunk-smiled. Head hanging and brushing my hair off my face, I thanked him and zigzagged to the car. Now, I had to see it a little more clearly. She wanted me to have an affair, to justify hers. I would not ever encourage someone to make a bad choice for herself, especially someone I loved. She didn't love me enough to protect me. She wanted to take me down. That was the first revelation of my best friend. In all the months of ambiguity, I saw her perfectly. Finally.

When I got home, Chad was sleeping. I felt dirty. I felt vindicated. Empowered and disgusted. It was rewarding to have him wonder where I was for once. Just once in all the years we were married. Always the dependable wife. Loyal. Always solid. Honest. He knew that the day he married me. Too dependable. I never spoke to that guy again, though I saw him in passing once.

Ryan and I met for lunch in a parking lot. I parked my car, and he got in.

"I'm in a funk," he began. "Trying not to be negative, but ..."

"I know. He still acts sneaky and mean—cold, mostly. Like the other night, he said he had to get his car washed at ten o'clock on a Tuesday night, because his boss was coming. Do I look stupid to you? If I questioned it, he got *really* mad. Like I'm a nagging wife."

"That's the night Caroline flew in from a work trip."

"What time did her plane come in?"

"She said it was late, so she didn't get home 'til midnight."

"Okay. Then that's where he was. I even drove like a crazy person to the closest carwash. I'm such an idiot. I didn't want to believe it."

"You know, I'm such a family guy, I would never work late like Chad does. Why doesn't Caroline appreciate that I even golf super early on Saturdays so I can be with the family? I don't gamble. I don't really drink. I don't smoke. I don't do drugs. I'm loyal. I'm nothing if not loyal. We have a beautiful home and a boat. We come from good families. I don't think I'm a bad looking guy. Am I?" He started laughing in some embarrassment. He continued. "Really. Our kids are perfect. What's so bad about our life? Really? I mean, am I so *terrible*?"

I laughed. "Of course not. There's something messed up inside them." I could have cried for Ryan. He looked like all that his heart had tried to be and do was eliminated by her actions. His eyes watered. This funny, ultra-intelligent, solid, athletic, family man loyalist.

I looked down at my sandwich. A tear dropped from my chin. "I don't know how to say this, but we have been so broken since Malak died. *Why*? *Why* did she pick *my* husband who is so *lost*? He's all I have left of the life I had besides Grace. What is broken in her that would make *her* leave a normal, good life for an already drowning one? Doesn't some part of her know how ruined he is?"

"He's so cocky," Ryan said.

"What do you mean?" I looked up.

"When he raced against me in the kayaks on vacation. Pompous. Like he was showing off for Caroline."

"Oh. Yeah. Sorry. That was bizarre. And way out of line." We were quiet for a second, looking at each other. Then I said, "Chad's lucky I don't go Kathy Bates in *Misery* on him."

"Yeah. He should watch his back."

I sighed. "I have to get back to work, Ryan. Will you keep me posted on what you know? If they keep this up, I have choices to make."

"Definitely."

We kissed each other on the cheek with a long hug.

"I'm sorry this is so horrible," I said. "Thanks for meeting me."

"Hang in there. You look great. Try not to let it get to you." He smiled.

"You too. I wanna see some skip in your step. You're an incredible dad and husband." I smiled back. He was such a good man. A kind person. Excellent communicator. Family guy. Very handsome. I guess you can't make sense of people's choices.

Goodness is not something I can do but a growing capacity for God in me. The longer we live, the more likely some version of torment will creep in. This teaches us that perfect behavior is impossible, but God has no remembrance of our errors or the shame we attach to it.

CHAPTER 14

I'm Fine

I dialed the phone.

"Hi. It's ten o'clock at night, and your husband is preaching tomorrow, but you've invited me over several times, Kate. Can I come over?"

"I'm so glad you called. Yes, yes, yes! Come over."

What a relief to hear those words from the pastor's wife, Kate.

I arrived with puffy eyes, and I carried a stash of tissues in my arms. I wondered—if the house could talk, would it lock the doors, protecting the dwellers inside, keeping them safe from what I brought with me? If it could hear, too, what stories must be told in these walls. I knocked meekly on the door, knowing their four children were already in bed. Kate's welcoming hug and smile greeted me before I stepped into the foyer. She led me to the den, dimly lit with one small lamp and two candles. It was calming and peaceful. She had done this before.

"I'm sorry; I am a mess," I murmured. With a self-deprecating giggle, I added, "I am a walking tribute to the success of a total frontal lobotomy!" We laughed in low levels so as not to wake the house.

Kate, with true talented hostess flair, inquired, "Would you like coffee or a soda?"

"No, thanks. I'm on a strict liquid Bacardi IV diet since my lobotomy surgery." We laughed again.

She asked me the one question that started the flood of words and ideas, emotions, and questions: "How are you?"

I blurted out, "I know since the last time we talked, I told you I was worried about Chad. I know Pastor asked to see him, they met, and I know how much you care about him. But he's a ... a different person. In all honesty, I sat with my trusted pastor, swearing like a sailor. I think he's having an affair, but he doesn't admit it. I can't help myself right now. Please forgive me." I started crying. Embarrassed by my anger, my lack of grace toward Chad, and fueled by my love for him and my hurt, it was a complete meltdown.

I cried, cussed, apologized. I made allowances for the man I loved, attempting to demonstrate mercy and grace for him. I loved him and hated him, and I had told him as much. Was I assured by his actions that he hated me? What was I to make of it all? Kate listened without judging either of us, which I really appreciated. I liked talking to someone *who loved Chad* too. I felt purged of my true shortcomings and helped by her compassion. She confided her own struggles in life and in marriage. We laughed about some of our idiosyncrasies. She prayed with me while I dissolved into tears.

"Sometimes, the curb looks like a step up in the world, a mountaintop even," she said. "When you feel like you've sunk lower than dirt, the pavement level would seem a promotion in status." We laughed. "Do you love him? People grieve differently. I can't imagine your pain, but in the end, we are here for you," Kate said genuinely. "We *are* praying for you both."

"Yes, I do, but this is getting more difficult, and I'm not sure I have the ability to see it to the end. It's killing me. I think I will talk to him again and see where we are."

Where was my strength to leave Chad? I recognized that my enabling spinelessness was an unsavory trait. Self-discovery was not a celebration. Something was different with Chad. I couldn't change his heart. So at the club, I chose to be selfish with that guy. I suppose that's how people get to this point. I borrowed love, if from a perfect stranger. Somehow, I was failing too—and was so furious about failing.

I would have a conversation with Chad the next time we were alone.

I took the first opportunity—the next day, Sunday, at 3:00 p.m., while sitting at the kitchen table. Grace was playing at a friend's house. My voice twitched as I told him, "I am afraid that if some nice guy asked me to lunch, I would go, Chad. Is that where we are? Is that how you feel? Because it's okay. Just tell me what you want."

He looked mad. He closed the sliding glass door right next to the table. "The whole world can hear you!"

I was being nice. Honest. Kind and very serious. Why was he mean? "I think the whole neighborhood knows we are falling apart, Chad."

"Don't overuse my name." he said. He was right. I did that when I was angry.

"Remember, we promised each other before we said 'I do' that if it ever got bad that we would leave first, before disrespecting the other person?"

He didn't respond.

He didn't say yes or no.

Looking back, it's baffling that I didn't push him harder on the subject.

"Do you? Do you want …" he asked.

"No. But … if that's where we're headed, then …"

"I don't know."

"Are you having an affair?" I asked again.

"No. Are you?"

"*No!*" Silly question. "Just move out, Chad."

"What? No way."

We left to separate rooms. Chad to his office. Me to the kitchen. Suspicious, I checked out his car to find something that would explain his behavior. I frantically shuffled through paper, in the compartment between the seats, under the seats, and in the trunk. But in the glove box, I found a book on personality disorders—not what I expected at all. I was searching for drug use, proof of the unexplained, the affair, anything. But absolutely *not* a psychological book that suggested an evaluation.

I called my counselor, Ms. T.

"Hi, I'm not sure … uh. I found a book on borderline personality disorders in Chad's car. Why … why do you think it's in there?" I told her the name of it.

She paused. "Where do you think he got it?"

"I'm reading some of it, and it's scary. Is this about me? *Am I crazy?*"

"No, everyone has some characteristics of this condition, especially when you've been through trauma like you have experienced. But I don't believe you fit this diagnosis."

"Honestly, Ms. T, if I have anything close to this form of mental illness, you need to test me and tell me. After everything else, if I'm actually mentally ill—and I wonder sometimes—then I will sign Grace away to Chad willingly. She's been through so much, so if I'm the only one who *doesn't know* that I have this condition, tell me now!" I crashed into blubbering.

Just the suggestion triggered more of my own inconsistencies and self-doubt.

"Do you think his counselor gave it to him?" she asked.

"I hope not! I went to the counselor with Chad—this man attends my church. I have told him that Chad was having an affair. I told him other concerns, while Chad was sitting there. It was as if his counselor thought I was lying. Chad was super calm. Oh, my gosh. I bet Chad told him I was compulsively lying. His counselor even asked if I had any evidence!"

"Let me call this man. With your permission, I would like to have a conversation with him. Is that okay with you? I am disturbed he has not had a conversation with me directly in the best interest of accuracy and in the best interests of both our patients. It is unethical."

"Yes. Please."

An hour passed before she called back. When I asked how it went, she said, "Don't worry about it. There will be no evaluation. You are fine."

"Thank you so much," I gushed. "I don't know what I would do without you. You keep me sane. Sometimes it's hard to keep it together and … thank you. Bless you."

"You're welcome. Take care."

That evening at nine o'clock, Chad's car pulled into the garage. He walked directly to his office.

I followed him and confronted him. "Really? You painted me as mentally ill? Where'd you get *that* idea? That was a new low, even for you." I was whispering now. "Of all the things that have gone down, that … is … unbelievable. I know you don't really believe that." He stared at the floor, and I walked out.

Simply to spite Chad and to gain peace, I left. Sleeplessness and discontent chased me out of bed at midnight. Chad locked his office door. In my lavender silk and lace lingerie, underappreciated, I shimmied jeans on underneath. Sneaking down to the garage, I glided on my leather jacket, with the lace peeking out the bottom edge. I slipped into a pair of easy heels. My hair was tousled, pinned up in a clip. Opening the garage door, I got into the car and pulled out into the black night air. Driving to the first gas station, I purchased my skinny menthols, a large coffee with vanilla creamer, sweetener, and a lighter. Back to the car, I lit up, took a sip, and decided where to go. For hours. Once in a while, I visited the elementary school at 2:00 a.m. There, where Grace's handprints were cemented in at the base of the green park bench installed in Malak's honor, I lay curled up on my side. My breath was the only warm anything, in the cold, I was content to cry quietly. So content on that bench, with the cigarette smoke lilting up and my coffee on the ground. I looked at the stars. Turning on my other side, my swollen eyes were cooled by the metal seat. I stayed there until I felt peace again. I reminisced about the parents and kids that showed up to install this bench in his honor. The cards each of the kids made about what they liked about Malak. All the green balloons that were given out to the kids to hold for the memorial ceremony. I don't remember a single word. I ignored it for the pain's sake. The school planned it all. I just showed up. The balloons were released with messages attached. Hugs from parents I had never met, with their stories of Malak. Tears on their children's faces. I sat with the Kleenex, smiling through my snotty nose. Could it be sweeter? More bitter? So the bench was my safe place. No one to answer to. No one to come find me. Malak and I could feel close. I scooped up my sanity, imagining a blanket thrown down from the sky, restoring my core composition somehow. There, I lay still on the bench in fetal position, with my hand raised to the night sky, as I had done before, wishing on his kisses. I grabbed God by clawing at Him in desperation. If I could somehow hold on to the neck of God with both hands, He would know how much I wanted to hold on to faith. I had to get God's attention. Make Him do a miracle. I wondered if the neighbors watched from behind the curtains. I sat up, straining to make out such a set of peering eyes. *Please let me be.* I worried they would see me for the crackpot I was. It was empty and filling at once.

After that, I drove to a golf course parking lot near our house. I stared at the moon and talked to God. I let the heater run with the window down, allowing the cigarette smoke to escape. I sat quietly. Then crying. Then laughing to myself about the ridiculousness of it all. I pounded the steering wheel in frustration and then rested my head there. Thirty minutes passed. I got out and sat in the grass. Lit up another cigarette. I asked God so many questions. Why? What should I do? We had conversations about what to do next. Had I let God down? What had I done? How could He? Help me with my angry, bitter symphony. Change me. Talk to me. Just talk *to me.* Why … why … why? Who are *You*, God? How can I become an incredible woman? Useful. Significant. Purposeful.

I was up all night; now it was a cold Sunday morning at six o'clock. Haggard. Messy hair. A face plastered by dried tears and smeary black mascara with bulbous eyes, I decided to fill the gas tank on my way home to shower and get to 9:00 a.m. church. Hoping to avoid anyone, I ducked behind the pump. I shivered and hid my face in my jacket. I bent over to pick up a penny. I smiled. I turned around to put the nozzle back into its place—and Jack, the nurse practitioner, was standing there. I laughed and apologized for my underwhelming appearance. *Great.*

"I've been up all night. I smell like coffee and cigarettes. I'm so embarrassed and in my pajamas." I laughed. "I was hoping no one would see me."

"Actually," he said, "I'm kinda embarrassed to say, I saw this woman's heels in a pair of jeans, with the lace hangin' out the jacket, and I said to myself—nice. But I didn't know it was you! Whoops!" Now we both were laughing. A tribute to his career, he no doubt had mastered the gift of making people's most personal traumas and embarrassments a comedy. Instantly, I was at ease.

"Chad is having an affair," I blurted. "It's been less than ... I will be fine, it's just ... been hard." I smiled, holding back the tears.

After a small pause, he asked me, as if he already knew, "With someone from work?" No smile on his face now.

"Yeah. You ... *know.*" My voice fell off.

"I was guessing." He seemed quietly nonjudgmental but sympathetic.

Jack was a great friend of Chad's, and Jack's wife was a gem. Neither of us continued the conversation.

"Thanks. You made me laugh, and I can't tell you how great that is." I sighed in huge relief. I turned to get back into my car.

His voice lowered and laughing, he said, "You know, if Katie Couric came to my office and asked me to have dinner with her, that would be it. I'd leave my wife in a minute, but not for anyone else, and my wife knows it!" He laughed again. "I don't think Katie's coming for me, though." His head tipped back, laughing. I think that was his way of saying that guys are *jerks*, but Chad loves me. That people are fallible, but that I was a good woman.

I smiled one last time. I knew he felt sorry for both Chad and me. "Tell your lovely wife thank you for the silver locket necklace you sent to Grace. What a very special, amazing gift."

"Aw, you're welcome!" he called out and got in his car.

That encounter was significant, because it was one day of sorrow that stuck out. I don't show my damages to the public, but he saw me. Smoky-smelling, run over, and massively rejected, I couldn't have hidden my misery if I had tried. Life had beat the crap out of me. I had searched for God all night long, waiting for Him to show up and talk to me. I guess God did, in the laughter and the smallest encouragement from a family friend—a divine appointment at the gas station. At my lowest point, He showed up.

I had been committed to my life preserver, my psychologist, Ms. T. I had been seeing her since Malak died, nearly every week, but of late, sometimes twice a week. She gave me my confidence back. Helped me manage my crisis. I couldn't wait to see her. She gave me measurable progress in decisions, and she facilitated clearer mental processing and practical plans to move forward.

Caroline invited me to lunch, and in some compulsory way, I went. I don't have any idea why. They had denied any affair and of course, I had no evidence, despite my tangled relationship with Chad. Maybe she had a reason to talk to me. Maybe she wanted to give up information. Or apologize. Maybe we would have a showdown. Opening the menus, we greeted each other, testing the barometric pressure. We ordered our Diet Cokes and water, as was customary. Down went the menus. With her hand on my arm, the standard head tilt, and her smiling eyes, she said, "I have been worried about you. How are you doing?"

"Um. I've been better." *Really. That's how this is gonna go?* This was a mistake. (*Super crappy, thanks,* I'd like to have said. *On second thought, I have more cuss words here than I dare admit. Let me scratch your eyes out. What are you asking me for in the first place?*) Was she repentant or goading me? Goading, I suspected. Was she on a mission in manipulation? What was I doing here?

Then again, if she *were* blameless, she would want to see me. Ugh.

Was her question simply served up as camouflage for her to determine whether I was accepting her denial of the affair? Or was she testing the waters to see if I knew of her relationship with my husband?

She wiped the tears on her face, in sadness for me in that restaurant. I could not find the circumference of the thing. Surely, she wouldn't justify. What was her perspective? Did she love him? I supposed. How could I figure this out? She was not a dumb woman. She must have decided I was an idiot to come here. I began to see that the longer it took me to believe it, the more mockery there was in her behavior.

I threw out a random stupid statement out of desperation and confusion. Why I didn't just ask her if she was having an affair, I can't say. Maybe

I was afraid if she said yes, I would lose my temper. Maybe if she said no, I wouldn't believe her. I was frozen. "You can have him. He's such a mess; you have *no* idea." She never gave an admission.

That was as close as we got to any genuine conversation. We left as uncomfortably fraudulent as we arrived. To be fair, we had missed each other's friendship, not to be confused with the abhorrent toxicity of it. She had been one of my best girlfriends. I had cut her off.

I told her of his suicidal bent; she accused me of lying. At one point, she patted me on the head in a patronizing fashion—in show of her supremacy, I supposed. I cannot say. But that was telling of her ridicule. Cruel. I saw her with clarity, eventually, but it was a slow revelation. She was all about herself. At least Ryan and Chad didn't speak. *This was ludicrous, really.*

I called Ryan to meet for lunch that week. We met in a parking lot again. "How are you?" I asked, faking cheeriness as he got into my car, my only friend in the conspiracy.

"I've been better." His voice full of disappointment.

"Me too. I think they are having the affair still. I just can't prove it. I might get a private investigator. I can't leave him until I know something *solid*. The last few times we have met, it has really made me feel … safe and understood. I'm not alone in this horrible experience …" My voice trailed off.

"I know. I don't talk to anyone about this, because it's too personal, and I'm glad we have each other. The stable ones. The sane ones. The stronger people. It really helps."

"Yeah. Thanks for your friendship. I'm sorry she did this to you. I'm sorry Chad got involved with her. It's all so hard to comprehend. I feel like we are living a crazy life we never asked for. What's wrong with them?"

Ryan laughed. "I've been thinking the same thing. Were their lives *so bad* that we drove them to this? I mean … I don't get it."

"Yeah, yeah." Laughing, I added, "I find myself second-guessing everything about myself. Do you?"

"Definitely." Hurt was evident in his voice.

"Sometimes he is unbelievably rude. Cold. Mean. I wonder if he hates me. I wonder what I've done."

"Caroline sleeps in the girls' room, or works late, or just doesn't talk to me."

"That sucks. I'm sorry."

"I don't get it. You're a great mom. An amazing person. You're intelligent and gorgeous. You and I are stable. Solid. That's so important. We are the stronger ones. We hold the fort down. Do the right thing. Keep the family going. He's never home. What's wrong with him? Who does that? Be a man, dude. Come on? Grow up. I don't get it. Don't take this to heart. He's a fool. Seriously. You know that, right?"

So very quiet in the car.

"Thanks. I *wish* Chad would be home for dinner every night like my dad was. That he didn't find some reason to be gone every weekend or that he just wanted to be … with us. It's always been that way. I hate that he's made reasons to not be home for most of our married life, but I tried to let it go. You're always home. Doing family things. Weekends with your family. Trips and outings. I've been begging to have him home and begging him to be with us … and now with our son's death … you would think, of all people, Chad would recognize how important we are to him. It's so obvious that we mean nothing to him at all."

He took my hand as I dissolved into tears.

"I'm so sorry." His face was full of emotion to match mine.

"Thanks. Really. I'm okay. But thank you so much. You are such a really good guy. Solid retirement. Trips to Majorca. The Maldives. I think you should know … you should feel good about yourself too. I gotta take snake-hunting trips and pay for buffalo hunting licenses. Lucky me." I began laughing and crying.

We hugged each other as usual. This time, we both began crying. It wasn't looking good. Our tears buried in each other's shoulders. He put his hands on my face.

"You're perfect. Stay strong." He nodded.

He made sense of my pain, because he understood it. Life had recently taught me by experience that nothing was safe. Not relationships, not trust, not driving down the road. I'm not safe with girlfriends or safe from gossip. I cannot protect myself from much. But in that moment, Ryan was solid. And safe. Safe. Just for a moment.

His face was comfortably close and overwhelmingly safe. Reassuring. Protective. Honorable. Too close. Too comfortable.

We kissed. Totally inappropriate. Completely wrong. But two broken hearts in their ambushed state made for bad decisions. I had grown to genuinely care about this man.

"See you soon," he said.

"I'm thankful to you for helping me remember who I am, in this mess."

"We are amazing people," Ryan reassured me.

"Yes, you are." I sniffled. "Bye."

Of course, I felt like crap. What else could go wrong? I never saw that coming, honestly. I don't think Ryan did either.

A month later, on a steamy summer day, I was talking with the neighbors out on the lawn. I had just finished putting pesticide on the hostas in the yard to prevent a militia of snails. Within minutes, the dog began drooling profusely and then went into seizures. I called Chad, and he rushed Piper to the vet. Piper, the family mascot, was going to be fine, but it almost killed her. She licked the rocks until enough poison caused her near blindness, kidney failure, and near death.

I had killed my son and nearly my dog. What's more, I had to laugh; it made me want to order up an exorcism. After the fifteen hundred dollars in expenses and the doggie drama at the pet hospital, I dared to ask Chad if he was all right.

"Fine," he said, walking past me in the avoidance I had come to know and hate. He was visibly depleted.

I'm nowhere near fine. Something snapped in me. Stop pretending. Stop the poppycock. I would *make* him look at his denial. I would pound the truth *at* him, and he would have to see it. There once was a beating heart of intimacy inside his chest. I was ready to linguistically mince him. And I did.

"Your dog isn't *effing-fine*, your daughter isn't *effing-fine*, your wife isn't *effing-fine*, your job isn't *fine*, your marriage definitely isn't *fine*, and you, sir, are anything but *effing-fine*! Get a grip and get some help. If you can't do it for yourself or for me, do it for Grace—you know, the only child you have *left*?" Brutal.

No response. Deafening silence. He walked out.

The punishers and their hatred. Erased, I was. His tender center needed rescue, purging, and repairing the death within him. Both fragile. A shell of the confident person I once was. Joyless. Aimless. Guilty. I went deeper into the dark places I had never been in my life. I would never choose them, like rooms of darkness in a maze that seemed to run its course, a rat seeking the exit, forcing me through doorways and hallways. I wouldn't wish them on my worst enemy, even Caroline. Honestly, not even Caroline.

The actions I judge harshly, I will have an opportunity to commit one day. This, according to me, is almost certain. This might be both the humor of God and a divine lesson in my arrogance. And His mercy.

CHAPTER 15

Dirty Hands

I got a call from a girl I worked with for a mere four weeks. She left the job, and I hadn't seen her in about six months when her call came on my cell phone. I was standing in the pharmacy line, waiting for prescriptions. A long line of fidgeting customers stood around me. She knew of Malak from his hockey days, though I didn't remember her.

She had mentioned him once, on my first day on the job. She'd told me she was sorry he had died, that he had been fun to watch while he "grew into his skates," and that she missed seeing him. I'd shed a couple tears, as did she. When I gone back to my desk, I'd found a penny on it. No one had been at that desk for six months.

Now, I heard her voice on my cell phone. "This is Anna. You remember me?"

"Yes. What a surprise! How are you?"

"I have something strange to tell you. I hope you don't think I am weird, but it's been bugging me for a couple of weeks, and I had to tell you about it."

"Okay … sure," I said.

"I went with my sister to hear a speaker out of town. He is a psychic. Talks to the dead. She really wanted me to go, I was kinda nervous and really would never go otherwise," she told me.

I didn't know where she was going with this.

"There must have been five thousand people waiting to talk to this man. He stopped right in front of me. He looked at me and said, 'I have a little eight-year-old boy here. He says you know his mommy. Tell her she is the best mommy in the world, and that he is not mad.' I have been keeping this to myself, running it over in my mind. You're the only one I know who lost a son. It's gotta be you."

"Really?" I blubbered really loudly, in front of everyone in the pharmacy. The pharmacist glanced in concern, which reminded me to get a grip. This, coming from a woman I hadn't seen in half a year and really didn't know very well. I thanked her. Malak had said, "You're the greatest mommy in the world."

Walking to my car, I wiped my eyes. Bewildered by the experience, I shuffled it to the back of my mind, unable to know what to do with her story. It was comforting, sort of. I parked the car in the garage and walked toward the mailbox. I grabbed the first bill; it was the phone bill. I paid these automatically every month, without checking the list of calls, but something told me to review the calls Chad was making.

Calls from his home office number to another number. I didn't recognize it. Texts to her cell number. Six calls throughout the day to *her*. Twenty minutes at max on one call.

I immediately called Ryan to ask if he knew this number.

"Sure. That's Caroline's office number," he told me. "Why?"

"Of course. I was just looking at the phone bill. Chad's calling her from his office."

"How much?"

"Enough."

"Crap."

"Yeah."

He sighed in disappointment. "Thanks. I'll talk to you later."

"Definitely."

And he hung up.

I walked into the bedroom, where Chad was packing his suitcase. Who knows why, but I wrote six small love notes and hid them in his suitcase in different compartments. He left that night.

While he was away for four days, I stumbled upon a CD of songs that he'd made. I listened to it. Clearly, it was a compilation for Caroline, not for me. I called him around 7:00 p.m. on his second night in Kansas. Later, I called the Johnsons home phone, after I was sure the girls were in bed.

"Ryan? Is Caroline out of town?"

"Yeah, somewhere in Kansas."

"Chad's there too, and he did not answer his phone when I called at seven. How's things at your house? Girls good?"

"I'm gonna kill him."

"You know, it takes two."

"I'm gonna kill him," he repeated angrily.

"Don't. That's my baby girl's daddy. We lost enough. That's enough."

"I'll call you back. I'm calling her. She always calls me back."

Three minutes passed, and then the phone rang.

"No answer," Ryan said without preamble.

I tried Chad several times after that. He did not return my calls. All night.

When he returned home, I planned a Friday night movie date with my husband. How idiotic of me to pick a romantic comedy. It's a sweet romantic comedy about a woman who can't remember anything, including her love life. Her husband profoundly proves his love to her over and over every day. I buried my face in the couch cushion through the whole thing. The movie only served to illustrate the selfishness of what we had become. The futility. Chad's complete lack of love for me.

An hour into the movie, in misery, Chad yelled, "Stop it. Stop it! I can't take it anymore." Not so much in anger but in compassion, his own burning hurt resonating in his words.

"I've been looking at the phone bills," I told him. "You talk to her about eight times a day. Grace said she came over here in the middle of the day to bring free circus passes given away by the grocery store. Really, Chad? You can lie to Caroline. You are good at it. If you can do it to me, you can do it to her. Don't talk to Caroline for a week—let's see if you can even do it. Tell her you're busy. Tell her it's family dinner, tell her you have to work, *anything*. But don't talk or text or see her. Can you do that? Can you?"

He nodded and looked at the floor.

I went to bed quietly. The next morning, I left for a workout and didn't return all day. It was the first time Chad had been responsible for Grace on his own. Sad but true. He had never had her for an entire day in ten years. I loved it. I didn't answer my phone. I didn't answer a text—unless I felt like it. It was an amazing, liberating feeling. He was in *my* place for the first time in our marriage, waiting for me to take Grace off his hands and grant him *his* independence. For years, he had done as he pleased, and I picked up the slack.

I received his text: "When are you coming home?"

I didn't answer.

He sent another: "When are you coming home? What are you doing? Just call me."

Five hours passed before I responded with my text response: "When I feel like it." Eventually, I called him. "Chad. I need time to really think. I don't know if I want to be married. I'm working through ... some things. I don't have much else to say."

"Okay. Well, just ... come home."

I knew he was scared. Likely moving toward anger. I called a friend for advice on strategically planning my divorce.

That next week, God bless Chad, he honored my request. I asked him not to speak with Caroline for five days. I could tell he hadn't called her, because Grace kept spilling the beans that Caroline was dropping by the house in the middle of the day while I was working. Wednesday evening at six, the phone rang. It was one of Chad's other female coworkers.

"Hi, how are you?" she said to me. "I haven't talked to you in a long time. What's new?"

"To what do I owe the pleasure?" I wasn't warm. She was good friends with Caroline. I happened to know that this woman was having an affair. I wasn't sure what this was about.

"Actually, I was trying to get a hold of Chad. He didn't answer his phone. Is he available?"

"He fell asleep on the couch with Grace. Can he talk to you tomorrow? I don't wanna wake them? If he wakes up, I can have him call you."

"Okay. Great. Thanks. Bye." Odd and short.

An hour or so later, Chad woke up.

"Chad, your other coworker called—Brenda. She wants a call."

He dialed her. He sounded uncomfortable, telling her he had to go, that we were having family dinner. He hung up.

"Ryan, quick question," I said when I next called him. "What was your wife doing last night?"

"She was out with Brenda, having a glass of wine at art class."

"Oh."

"Why?"

"Because she had Brenda call the house to talk to Chad so she could get on the phone to talk to him. I had asked him not to call her or talk to her for a week. So she's calling the house, with Brenda's help."

That Saturday, when my parents came to town, Caroline showed up at the house, uninvited. I actually hugged the woman who used to be welcome and walked her to the door, explaining that we had company. Under my breath, I said to my stepmom, "That woman is sleeping with my husband, and she was one of my best friends."

The surprise on her face was priceless. "My, she has a lot of nerve, doesn't she?" she said, her brows reaching peak performance.

I said, "Oh, they don't know it yet, but I will be busting them."

Chad decided to show my parents his garden a few miles from our house, where you rent a plot. Unfortunately, he created and shared it with Caroline and another work partner. It had become a source of contention for me because he made me feel like I couldn't plant anything there, not that I had been a gardener anyway.

"Do I have the right to pick a couple of Caroline's flowers?" I asked my stepmom.

"Certainly. If she thinks she has the right to sleep with your man, I think you can pick as many flowers as you would like!" she said with a cheery smile. We did snicker, I will admit. When I asked Chad for his trusty pocketknife, the idea seemed to make him nauseated. I cut a big bunch, leaving tall, bare stems standing two feet high in the glorious section of flowers. No one ever said retaliation wasn't fun. Unfortunately, most of the flowers died before we got home that day. A few made it to a small vase.

Later that night, I had time alone with Chad. I kissed him on the forehead and whispered, "Thank you for choosing me today. I know that must have been hard, but thank you. I love you. You didn't get up to greet her when she stopped over. You even looked uncomfortable."

"Really, honey?" Relief was in his voice.

"Yes." I said, and we kissed for a moment like we used to do. But I would never know if he really chose me. Within a few days, he wouldn't have a choice anymore.

Ryan and I met more frequently as our own affair became more intense, sharing updates and information in order to catch them. But the rejection pain lessened—temporarily—the more we kissed. That first kiss with Ryan had moved to a few kisses and then to a full-blown—however short—affair. I am both mortified and ashamed of my choice, but I came by it quite unintended, as I supposed Chad had. Ryan meant the world to me at the time. We had become great friends, and he offered some tangible comfort where the serrated blades had cut our hearts. However disappointing our marriages had become, and our poor choice, it was true nonetheless.

"Ryan, I can't do this anymore, we are just as bad as they are! I've hated Caroline. For a year now, I've hated her like I've hated no other person. Now, I'm her, and I can't be that!" My words became garbled words as they spilled from my mouth in awkward regret. "I refuse to be *that*. I've always been proud of making the right decisions, even when no one is looking, Ryan. My family is so messed up. Grace would never be the same, and I don't want to see Caroline one more time, much less if we truly started a relationship—and that's ... more bizarre than—"

"I know," Ryan said, his puppy eyes full of tears.

"I don't want to be *this girl*, and honestly, I don't want *you* to be that kind of a man. We owe our kids and ourselves that kind of character. I don't even know who I've become. You've been the safest, kindest, most honest part of my ... but I can't *justify* it. Can you imagine the gossip? Let's keep this a secret. If we do the right thing, then that's what's important. They didn't do the right thing. If they had, we wouldn't be here."

"Wait. This never would have happened if they hadn't broken this marriage in the first place, and you know it!" he said bluntly.

"Yes. I never even—no offense. This is ... such—"

"We ... never would have been here, and you know it."

I nodded.

"Nothing mattered after that," he said. "It was already busted."

Sadly, I hated the truth. I blamed myself for not being a better person. I think if Chad had ever come clean and made a choice, earlier than all the collateral damage, maybe it would have been different. "Ryan, I'm gonna fix this mess. I'm calling a private investigator."

I decided to draw a line to stop the craziness. I arranged for the PI to arrive on the day I had planned elective surgery. I was turning forty and had opted to have a couple of additions put on the old girl. I would be gone all day, sixty miles away. Perfect opportunity. If they wanted one.

Caroline had come over to bring me Godiva chocolates, plenty of magazines, hugs, and a kiss with well wishes. *Please*. This was almost fun. She sat across my kitchen table, not knowing what I knew. I knew she had come by a lot recently while I was at work. I had to face it. She knew nothing of the phone bills, the private investigator, or how much I was tracking their activity. She was playing poker, as usual, but I finally got the house straight. She handed me a congratulations card. Curious.

It is incredible what lies—literally lies—beneath the surface. The card puzzled me at first. "To Cinderella in the castle, with the handsome prince and all the shoes"—"shoes" was crossed out, with "boobs" scribbled in its place—"that she could want."

What was there in someone like me, who had lost so much, to admire? To the point that she was jealous? Why would anyone in his or her right mind envy me? What about my life would anyone want to steal? Now I saw her competitive nature and the jealousy in that one card. I could not imagine. I'd never seen her motive—until then. I must have been blind. She was calculated. Narcissistic.

I noticed something most peculiar. Caroline was staring over my shoulder to the windowsill behind me. Intently. Nervously. Was she annoyed? I couldn't let my snide smirk give me away. Caroline was *very* distracted but did not want to get caught at it. I had my back to the window, so I turned to look and then glanced back at her face. How poignant—me, watching her, watching me. She seemed bright green!

A few flowers remained from the day I had cut them and placed them in that small vase on the windowsill. Vengeance without intent. Evil and divine. I could tell that Caroline was trying to decide if Chad had picked *her* flowers for *me*. Or had I had the audacity to cut her flowers for myself, without asking. I think it was the former. Either way, this didn't sit well with her. She didn't say a single word. I walked her to the door; the PI was at his post. "You're fired, Caroline ..." I mumbled under my breath.

As Caroline backed out of the driveway, I memorized her license plate and called it into the PI as requested. The end was in sight. I would be free from lies. Everyone has a story. Silly that I considered myself immune from weakness and tragedy. Once, Pollyanna. Now, my life was expelled in a devil's burp, after two years of burning indigestion.

The PI confirmed my suspicions by naming meeting locations and times that were clearly covert in nature. I didn't need any other convincing. I took a deep breath. I called Ryan. It was a short, quiet conversation.

Ironically, that same evening Chad and I were scheduled to meet at his sister's house near the surgery center. He wanted to go on a date for dinner. *Too late*, I thought.

At Chad's sister's house, every woman in the family was curious about my surgery. Even Grace had questions, but not Chad. I pulled him into the bathroom. In a singsong, sweet n sick way, I asked him, "What's the matter, Chad?" I was ruthless and mean-spirited. "Everyone but you wants to see the landscape changes post-surgery?" Nothing like a woman scorned. I couldn't believe he didn't want to see them. I began to reveal the purchase, one button at a time. He stood in front of me, staring, speechless, like a deer in headlights. His hands were out to the side like he was afraid to touch me. Since when?

"Don't you want to feel them?" I asked. "Everyone else has."

"My hands are dirty."

There it was. Finally. The first admission. Suspended silence. He heard himself say it.

"You're d*** right they are." I glared at him and buttoned my shirt. This, with our families outside the bathroom door. I left the room. The families knew nothing. The pivotal hour. It was poetic justice that the revelation of the affair took place in a bathroom at the Bermuda resort and found closure in a bathroom in his sister's house. It was such a relief; we should have done this a long time ago.

Chad tried to have a date night with me, but I was ice. Nice, like I would be nice to a stranger on a bus to nowhere, but that was it. I didn't know him anymore. I would have given anything to find something familiar about him. I will admit that I wanted to be with my husband one more time, without his knowledge of its being over. The man had been my love, my babies' father. I was sure of the loneliness to come. Freedom is priceless, but it would cost me everything I had loved.

The next morning, he was whimpering in his sleep. This, I used against him. I told him he was crying in his sleep and mumbling. Admittedly, I was celebrating my revenge. I took the shot and had no guilt about it. He was skittish. He sat up, and his voice jumped two octaves as he asked, "What did I say in my sleep?"

Without expression, watching him, I let the silence irritate. What made him sweat over it? Where, after all the ruinous months, where was this remorse coming from? Motivated by my sinful satisfaction, I answered his question with, "Oh, I don't know. I didn't get it at all. No big deal." I'd torture him. I loved this, unfortunately. "You were crying about ..."—I paused again—"Malak. I think." This was punishment, more than I'd imagined. Visibly fidgety, he was very uncomfortable. What *had* he dreamed? It played out like observing his symbolic burial in the relationship. I knew somehow, he feared calling Caroline's name in his sleep. He had been watching all *my* responses, but for the first time, I tested and watched *him*. He kept his phone in the bathroom with the door as he showered. A red flag. This would not end unless I made it stop. An hour later, pushed to the brink, he sighed every three minutes.

I found him at the kitchen table. His forehead was resting on his forearm on the table as he rocked side to side. It did make me smile—I am not holy or blameless. I was in his shoes for the first time, and I felt so malicious, yet validated. Liberated. In control of the puppet strings for a change.

"Honey, what's the matter?" I asked him, like the lying, sneaky snake I had become.

"Nothing." His typical reply, but he was miserable. I wondered if Caroline was chewing him out on the other side of the mountain. I wondered if she was pressuring him to take a stand.

I sat on it for two weeks.

Why? I was digesting the past and considering the future. Watching for signs of something to hold on to. Killing my hope for reconciliation a day at a time, until I had enough courage to *do* something, rather than lie in limbo. He never admitted to an affair, really, other than the one-liner, *my hands are dirty.*

While sitting in an empty parking lot, I picked up the phone and dialed my lifelong protector for his advice. "Daddy, how do ... you know when to end your marriage? How will I know?"

"You will know, honey. If you're not sure, don't do anything. But you will *know*." As he had taught me so many times, this rule applied to every decision in life, especially the big "page-turners." It's so simple. As always, Dad had wisdom.

"Love you, Daddy. Thank you."

Reaching my composure, I hung up. I dipped my head to see the sky out the front windshield. I prayed, "Lord, tell me how to do this. I just don't know how or why this happened. I need You. Help me to be wise, calm, sane, and clear-minded. In Jesus' name, amen."

I will die with words of hope on these lips.

CHAPTER 16

Courage

Short on words for the first time in my life and without an ounce of fight left in me, I considered my actionable steps. Slipped on a purple blouse, a spritz of perfume, curled my hair, and fixed my makeup. I wanted to look pretty for the last dance. I was taking back my self-worth and confidence. I would walk away, altered on the inside but with my head up. This was a landmark of sorts.

Chad and I had put incredible effort, time, and money into our marriage, so I wanted to finish strong, not pitifully. Not haggard, but captivating and brilliant. Sexy. Impervious. Awe-inspiring. Serene. Not beaten. Not defeated, angry, or bitter. I wanted it to be a *Life* magazine photographic moment of closure for me. A rare jewel of priceless value. This was a business transaction—that's all it was. I chose the bedroom, as it seemed both personal and appropriate in some distorted way. I wasn't sure if he'd react explosively or simply happy to leave me. I got my swagger on. It was two o'clock on Wednesday afternoon.

He answered his cell phone, and my words were, "Where are you?"

"I just had a meeting with clients."

"Who is with you?"

"Caroline and Kathryn."

"Come. Home. Now." I had a distinctly dead tone. He must have known my intentions. Neither of us had ever heard me speak so simple, pointed, and nondescript.

What should have taken him five minutes took forty-five—and two phone calls. It wasn't as if we hadn't expected this for months now. I heard the garage door open. He prepared his answers.

Sitting on the bed, I could hear his steps on the curved staircase, reticent, thump … thump … thump. Sigh. Another sigh. And a pause at the top landing. As he entered the bedroom, I saw his tie was off, his posture drooping; he was resigned to his mistakes. No fight in him either. I was relieved. He offered no words. No denial.

I began the conversation. "We will get a divorce. You know why. We will be agreeable and go through arbitration and get this over as fast as possible. We will get along for Grace's sake. You need to move out this weekend."

He agreed. Sorrow and remorse for both of us. We had loved deeply. He exhaled. I exhaled. He said the hardest part was living a double life and that he hated himself for it. The facade had fallen. I had never seen him like that. I never knew how he felt, I had only seen his anger. The mean, darkened man was gone, and the guy I married sat on the bed, now recognizable. He seemed to think I couldn't love him with his hidden faults laid bare. The irony was, I would have in still greater measure.

We don't trust others to love us when we mess up. I traced his face and his hands with my eyes and my heart. For the first time, I realized I had not actually lost him to Caroline. He was lost to himself. That was huge. And incredibly sad, but it set me free from not being enough.

Typical of Chad's patterns of avoidance, he had already made plans to help re-roof a friend's cabin. He packed and left for the weekend. We did not speak for three days.

On his Sunday return, I called him a number of times. I got worried.

The phone rang at two o'clock Monday morning. I yelled at him for not returning my calls. He was cold at first. I asked him, "How hard is it for you to just politely communicate with me and tell me what your plans are? We are getting a divorce. Can you just communicate?"

Niagara Falls spilled over. Mount Vesuvius erupted. "I want to drive off the road! I'm so miserable!" His anguish gushed over for the first time.

I was scared. "You need help, honey. Just promise me you will get home. I won't leave you. You have to get help as soon as you get home. Promise?"

"Yeah." He sighed in relief. "Okay," He said, with a couple of tears left.

He arrived home in the morning hours, as promised, called his boss, and asked for a leave of absence. He lay on the floor of his office, curled up in fetal position from his self-hatred and ultimately in sadness for losing control of his life. I realized that the Chad I knew would never allow himself the slightest show of such physical and emotional weakness, much less this collapse. I took his hand and led him into the bedroom, where he fell fast asleep. He asked me to stay and hold his hand. I did. I had always been afraid of my own emotional demise, not his. He was bold, blunt, opinionated, strong, and cocky even, it seemed to me. I understood for the first time how this had eaten at him.

His mom was on her way to pick him up. I had gotten a new job, and I couldn't stay home with him. Once Chad's mom arrived, I left for work, but I was torn. I told his mom I couldn't save him; I didn't know how.

Chad, to his credit, left for a clinic out of state to treat his depression that day. With tremendous courage and eight hours a day of therapy, he received radical counseling for depression that aided him, so he could swallow his world in digestible pieces.

I saw phenomenal changes through his therapy, but there was still Caroline. She left a trail of undying attempts. She saw this as an open door. Bless him; he was honest about it, swayed by her, because he loved her but didn't want to be with her. Or be alone, should I leave him. Caroline pursued him by phone in treatment, complaining of her unhappiness, while Chad had homework every night for the sessions each day.

Chad's honesty was coming back. He returned from his month-long treatment, and within three days, he asked me to go to a therapy-appointed counselor with him. "Tell the counselor all the lies," he begged me. Brave, brave man.

I was so angry and tender underneath those lies; I wasn't sure what would happen.

I maligned the man—worse, I gave him a horrific flogging, by regurgitating his many "sins." He just nodded and buried his head in his hands. What an act of unselfish repentance. It was dreadful for him, cleansing for me. I branded him the unpardonable man. It took valor in character for Chad to sit through all that, willing to be a better man, and I beat him up with it. I couldn't help myself. The point of this exercise was to determine whether there was anything worth saving after all. The counselor asked me if I could try again. That was a question I hadn't expected. Chad sat listening, as if he had been afraid to ask me himself.

"Um ... I don't think I will be able to really trust him. He has been so cold for so long. I couldn't do that ever again. It was too damaging for me. I begged him to love me, way before all of this. You can't love someone and ignore her. I refuse to beg anyone ever again to spend time with me. I'm afraid of who I would become. Punishing him. I don't like who I've become already. I barely survived this. I have graphic images in my head of her and—I … can't. I'm sorry. I'm so sorry."

Later, he stood in our bedroom hall, looking at me with a gentler, kinder glance. I was almost uncomfortable. "Let's just move. Anywhere. Anywhere you want—far, far away if you want."

I had just completed three weeks of peace in his absence—not wondering who Chad was talking to or where he was, which made my slumber sweeter. What if I had a rifle to his chest six months from now, when I discovered he had been with her, or he missed her?

That makes me sound violent and unglued, but I was all too close to my limit. I acknowledge that. I feared who I would become. I remember sliding down the wall to the floor, my hands hiding my face, realizing I couldn't let him in again.

"I know this is painful," I told him, "and I wish it weren't true, but I can't … I can't. It is finally peaceful here." I couldn't put Humpty Dumpty together again.

Faith had begun to separate us too. My faith had become huge to me. I wanted intimacy, even in the church pew. We changed in our trauma to somewhat different people. He had his own race to run. He was remarkable in many ways.

At a favorite sandwich-and-salad restaurant, at an outside table, we laughed and talked, hiding the real reason for our family meeting. Chad winced throughout the conversation. Faking a good time, we tried to make it as enjoyable as possible to the last second. As we all held hands in a circle, Chad began, "Grace"—his voice cracked—"your mom and I love you very much. But … we are getting a divorce."

"Why, Daddy? Why? Why? *No! No!*" Gigantic tears were followed by screaming. "No … Daddy, no, no!"

After disrupting the restaurant, we left, harried. We found seats in the Suburban with the back gate doors open. Grace grabbed his neck, screaming and red-faced, "No!" Chad rocked her, her arms locked. In contrast to the glorious blue-sky Saturday, we all cried.

Any parents who have delivered the divorce truth to their children know the gravity of it. Chad paid in a sea of anguish. I did not envy him. He desperately wanted to tell his reason, to purge himself, but I shook my head. This kind of remorse, I had wished to see, but it left an indelible impression on my heart. If nothing else, his debts were canceled right then and there. I traced through the lines on his face as he hugged Grace, still rocking and rocking her for what seemed like hours, while the river ran, cutting and stinging his paper-fragile heart. His miserable guilt made me want to wash him in mercy myself, if I could have. It was a beautiful, awful moment. The release of lies, the pain of truth. Even my own uncovered guilt. It made me think of the times during the affair when he had watched Grace sleep and left me in an empty bed. It helped me realize that he loved her so, yet he couldn't reconcile himself to his error. There was my man, the one I'd been looking for all this time.

Grace wrapped herself around him as if he was leaving forever, even though he had left us a while ago. They buried their faces in each other's neck. Back and forth he cradled her while she cried. He patted her back, stroked her hair, and fought his tears.

"I'm sorry, baby. I'm so, so sorry."

Only kindness could flow from me, so I let them be, just the two of them.

He closed his eyes in such an expression of emptiness. I put my hand on my heart and looked at the sky.

Chad hurriedly purchased a house, but he stayed for a month in our home until his closing date. It was a roller coaster. One second, we missed each other, and the next, we fought. I rolled under the covers one night, only to find myself wondering where he was for three days afterward. So it went. But in early December, Chad enlisted good friends to help him move, and I helped. Our friends were surprised to see us get along so well, but we had done a *little* healing.

It was Christmas. I was living alone for the first time. The gloriously decorated shopping mall bellowed Christmas music, bows, and baubles. With heartache in my chest, I tried to enjoy it. Santa Claus. Blinking lights. Carolers.

I saw her. Her husband in tow. He looked nervous. The Johnsons were walking toward me as if I were a museum piece behind the glass. Four sets of eyes stared. Caroline glared at me. What was that? Ryan's look might have been fear that I would embarrass the family and expose the truth to his daughters. The two sweet angel girls smiled, which contrasted Caroline's cold stare. I had ignored her and put up with her sneering confidence for months. Not this time. Not like at the school fund-raiser, where she asked me how I was in front of all of our knowing neighbors. Or the time she said hi to me in our workout class, as if no one knew she was working out my husband that afternoon. Everyone held their breath to see if a brawl would start.

She liked throwing it I my face while everyone watched. Like in Macy's, where she had walked past me, come at me, looking for a fight with a blank face. We could have spit in each other's eye; we'd been so close in proximity. Afterward, I'd walked to a remote corner, hidden under a lower rack of women's clothing, with my tremors, rapid pulse, and racing respirations, feeling so demeaned and cowardly. I might have choked the crap out of her if I'd gotten close enough. Who conspires to dominate and conquer her best friend? My life was already broken. Geez, how hard was that to conquer? She was the only person who was more damaged than I was.

No. That was then. On this day, I was powerful. I stared back until she walked past. I could have used this opportunity to hurt her children. Embarrass her publically. Hurt Ryan. Even she had to know I was much better than that. Besides, the picture-perfect family wasn't happy, even if I was jealous that she had one. Her misery behind the façade was her own prison.

It was her way of saying, "If I can't have him, you can't have him either." I was a little amused. Caroline made a conscious choice to stay with her man, given plenty of opportunity, and Chad had seen this too. Nothing in her life changed with her mistake. It cost Chad everything. Grace and I paid plenty.

I will never understand Caroline. I think her wounds from childhood left marks on her, like most of us. Not that I am excusing her actions. I think her conscience was severed as a girl, when a mother who should have loved her was motivated by jealousy of her own daughter. Competitive. Caroline never got the skills to navigate her jealousies. She was able to teach confidence, love, support, and nurturing to her children, which was amazing, considering. No boundaries were taught to her, just self-motivated jealousies, where personal gains by any means would always support the outcome, regardless of the costs to anyone else.

I was no angel. Obviously. Sure, I wanted to lock her in the women's bathroom and bite her and beat her bloody and bald, but then, I'd lose my self-respect. Oddly, I couldn't see my affair with Ryan as the same, even though it was. Maybe that was denial, but it wasn't justice. Or in good character. Or correct. After everything I had managed to crawl out from under, that was my final undoing—I was disappointed that I had not lived stronger. The little reputation I had left as it was, in small town gossip circles. Nonetheless, in my humanness, I'd question her, but I felt I owed her the bridling of my accusations and mutilating words.

I, too, have inflicted harm, no less damaging. Lord, help me choose to be the wise woman I want to be. That it be well with my soul, my Savior, and everyone in my life, as well as those reading these pages. Humanness was not escapable. I think, too, that if Chad had known that I had had the affair, it wouldn't have bothered him. He seemed *that* distant to me emotionally, would it would have been inconsequential—except to justify his behavior. A complicated fabric of interwoven threads, with countless frays and repairs. But there was a golden thread.

To the best of my knowledge, the relationship between Chad and Caroline ran its course and ultimately deteriorated. I had heard rumbles of their activities, with ups and downs, but it was a relief to not concern myself with it anymore.

Three months after I asked Chad for a divorce, I ran into Caroline on the street. She stopped, tilted her head, and asked, "How are you?"

"I'm okay. It's been the hardest thing …" I winced a smile, leaning my head in the same fashion.

"Yeah," she said with nervous laughter. "It's been really hard."

It had been hard for *her*? Even if I should have given her credit for her honesty, I had no empathy. *It's not supposed to be about you, Caroline. It was never supposed to be about you. Oh, seriously, did you learn nothing?*

"But Caroline, it was two years of just Malak and then this … I can't even …" My face was emotionless. The fact that she was still clueless was devastating. *She never did wear those earrings*, I thought. *She said they hurt. I'll bet. Like guilt.*

"Yeah, and you still get out of bed, I know," Caroline said. No closure.

For Grace's sake and my own, I tried to keep the gossip quiet, but after a while, that was useless. You can't keep a roaring lion quiet in your hall closet either. I didn't add my own truths, because that would only serve to hurt more people.

"Did you wanna to come over tonight for wine with Sarah, Beth, and me?" It was Judy, from the neighborhood circle. I grew to fear her invites, because they went, as this one did, something like this:

"Uh, I'm tired," I said. "Maybe another time?"

"Then come and relax! Just for an hour?"

"Just for an hour."

I sighed.

When I arrived, the chardonnay was poured; veggies and dip were on the center island

"Have a seat. How are you?" Judy asked.

The other neighbors were already seated, and I heard murmurs of conversation and low-decibel laughter.

"How is everything? Are you doing okay?" Judy continued. The room got silent.

"Yeah. You know, I'm above ground." I laughed.

"Tell me what's going on? How are you and Chad doing? We worry about you."

"I get so angry with him for not getting help, mostly ..."

"What do you *mean*?" Judy looked like she was about to get the gossip.

You could have heard a pin drop. I fidgeted. I didn't want to talk about Caroline. If they knew, why weren't they telling *me*?

"Drink up; kiss and tell. We just care about you guys," Beth said sweetly. Scrupulous.

"I feel like I walk around with so much emotion shoved down. I'm angry; he's angry. He's so incredibly *mean* to me. It's like he can't stand me." *I'm not the one who screwed up,* I thought but kept it to myself, *How does he have the right to be angry while I cover for him?*

"Well, he seems good when we see him. I mean, he's been joking around and in good spirits." Judy prodded.

"You're the one who seems *so angry*? Wow." Mary's face looked like I was a mental hospital candidate for some reason. Was she judging my madness?

I wanted to scream the truth, but I would regret it, certainly. Everyone thought charming Chad was so perfect. It's like they thought I didn't deserve him.

Blurting out my anger, I said, "I am on-fire furious. Do you have a problem with that?" Defending myself. Do I have to defend myself? No.

I dropped a level to tears. *So tired of crying.* I felt manipulated. Criticized. How did I get myself in this dumb situation?

"Why so angry?" Judy pushed. They looked at me as if someone had told them that I was unstable. As if fury was a disease. As if I needed medication. As if they questioned my … sanity. Their mouths were hanging open. The hostess poured me another glass.

"No. I don't need—I need to leave. Yes. I have a ton of emotions. They are hard to manage. Thanks for having me over. I'm sorry. I have to go."

Why did I apologize? My parents taught me to be polite, and I guess I felt it would be rude not to answer. The truth was, I shouldn't have gone to Judy's house in the first place.

As soon as I got home, the phone rang. The caller ID showed it was Judy. I didn't answer.

She called three more times.

I didn't answer.

I listened to her message: "Please call me. You seemed upset."

I dialed the phone. "You know, don't you?" I said flatly.

"What are you talking about?" Judy asked in denial.

"You know."

"I have no idea," she lied.

"Yes, you do. Yes. You do, or you wouldn't have asked me over. You do, or you wouldn't have called repeatedly. You didn't get what you wanted."

"Tell me? What do you think I know?"

Another bold lie. Who tells the truth anymore? "About Caroline!" The bitter and childish whining squeaked out of me like I was a two-year-old. I was so humiliated. I couldn't bridle my tongue.

"Well, I have seen them over there barbequing. On your birthday. And she confided that you weren't doing well at all and that she was Chad's confidant."

"I bet." *Oh, my.* "Thanks for keeping this a secret for so long, Judy. Thanks for giving me the benefit of the doubt. Thanks for egging me on all these months over glasses of wine under the guise of being helpful. We are *not friends* anymore. I am sorry. You were a great friend to me in the past; you have done many unselfish things for my family. But let me be clear. I do not consider you a friend. You just kicked me when I was down. You have probably been talking about us for months, but you never said a thing."

"I didn't know for sure. I didn't want to hurt you."

"You heard I wasn't well, didn't you? You didn't even ask me. You assumed. And you knew. How could …" I took a deep breath.

I hung up.

Grace asked if she could write a letter. By herself. She asked me to review it for spelling errors only and to stay downstairs while she composed it. I corrected "perspective." That was the only change to its original structure. Grace was nine years old.

> *Dear Caroline,*
>
> *I am writing this letter, just me and neither of my parents.*
>
> *I just wanted to let you know how much I loved you. You were a really great person to me. Then one day, when I found out that you and my dad had an affair, it crushed me flat. I didn't know what to say. It really hurt to know someone I loved and cared about could hurt me that badly. You also (in my perspective) hurt yourself and everyone around you, such as the following: me, my mom, Ryan, Lilly, Eva, and so on.*
>
> *I don't want to throw this in your face, but I thought you should know what I thought. You have lost most of my trust. I have already given my dad a piece of my mind, so don't think I blame only you.*
>
> *Don't worry; I will never tell Eva or Lilly. I see Lilly every day, and one day Lilly asked me why you don't come to my house anymore. It really bothered me, and I went to the bathroom and cried.*
>
> *Did you think that by what you did after Malak died, it would make my family's life any better? Did you think about anyone else? I cried when I saw you the other day. I don't know what to do when I see you. When I see you, I would like it to just be a quick hi, how are you, and bye.*
>
> *Grace*

Caroline responded with a copy to Chad and me. I'm paraphrasing here, because we didn't save her e-mail in our disappointment, but she basically said that there were two sides to every story and that she didn't feel right saying anything further because of me. This implies blame.

"Mama? Why doesn't her letter just say *I'm sorry*? It seems like she's not sorry."

"Yeah. It would have been nice—and grown up—of her to just say I'm sorry."

Even a little girl can decipher honest repentance.

All of us have tapestries where the threads give way in areas that are unexplained. Say, for example, a new skirt with an imperfection. Imperfection coexists by necessity. At least in this world.

CHAPTER 17

The Twin

When the winter months set in, Grace retrieved her summer clothes from atop the closet shelf, so that she could pack a suitcase to visit my mom's beach house in South Carolina. She called my name. By her inflection, I knew it was significant. I found her on her knees, fallen, tears dripping like flooded memories and empty promises over the clothesbasket. Grace had found not one but two shiny 2006 pennies. It was 2006. I was without an explanation. The articles in the basket had been washed and put away months ago.

We arrived in South Carolina to my mom's beach house, where we had years of memories as a family. Mom hugged me, with the kind of infusion that heals. Nothing was better than seaside therapy. Or the art of eating. A well-known restaurant on the beach was the destination, a full hour away. I was tired, ornery, and hungry. I hate it when I know I've been rude but for some reason, I can't snap out of it.

Once we got there, we had to wait another forty-five minutes to be seated. We ordered an appetizer and an elixir to improve my mood. Three of us sat on a garden bench, watching the interesting crowd.

I spotted a boy that I guessed to be about five years old. He had white-blond hair in a bowl-cut. When he turned around, I saw bright blue eyes and the same cheeks I adored. I didn't take my eyes off him—I couldn't. Was I projecting something in my desire to see my son? Mesmerized, after two long minutes, I dared to look at Grace. She nodded, still gazing at him. She couldn't believe it. Mom noticed him too, inadvertently exclaiming, "Oh *my*!"

None of us said a word after that. We watched him walk, wiggle, and giggle. He struck a pose and smiled right at us with intent interest. His clothes—everything was so familiar. He was barely different somewhere in the face. I examined him with almost a twisted longing.

Grace pushed a lower-lip pout. Mom did the same. Could this child's mom read my thirst for the past in the reflection of her child? Against my own best interest, I was drawn in magically. "I have a son who looks so much like yours. He's precious." (I couldn't tell her he was dead.)

"Oh." She laughed.

Now I was nervous. *What did I just do?*

Mom stepped up this time. "This is Grace, I'm the grandma, and this is my daughter."

Smiling politely, she introduced herself.

I asked her, with a nagging curiosity, "What are your children's names?"

"This is Maxwell. We call him Max," the mother said.

My mom nudged me to take out Malak's picture from my wallet. That was a bad idea, wasn't it? What would I say next?

"Oh, *wow*!" the woman said in genuine amazement. "They really do look alike! What's his name?"

Laughter flowed freely eliminating tension for a second. Validation. *Even she thinks they look alike.* Her son ran around, stopped, looked at us, and then acted like he had seen a ghost. He disappeared off behind his father, twenty feet away. He was afraid of us. Did he know something? I didn't blame him.

"What did you say his name was?" The woman repeated her question.

I smiled. "Malak."

"That was going to be Maxwell's first name, but we decided on Maxwell Malak!" she flipped her hair as she laughed in surprise.

I choked. I looked down with an awkward grin. I had dropped my keys, nearly my liquor, but most notably my jaw. We avoided more conversation due to the impending discomfort for the unsuspecting family. I couldn't tell them. I would have to lie. She called Maxwell over to greet us, but he ran away, crying. The mom was apologetic, but we reassured her it was just fine. We closed the conversation, exchanging "nice-to-meet-yous." I sipped my liquid sedative.

I found a quiet spot outside the restaurant crowd near a smelly dumpster, foul as it was. I felt such a momentary rage that I almost thrust my glass at the pavement. I refrained, because ... because some poor soul would have to clean up my mess. I was always dependable. Appropriate. I was hurt and angry, but I chose self-control. I swept tears from my cheeks. Was this a gift of momentary joy or torment? On this side of heaven, I will not know. I left my tantrum with the other refuse stench and returned as a grown-up.

Later that night, home at the beach house, I tucked Grace in. In the warm breeze, moisture dribbled down her cheeks, and I whispered, "You are loved. You are special. You are intelligent. You are a gift from God. You are thankful and beautiful and peaceful. I love you, baby girl."

"Mama? Do you remember that time we were sitting at dinner, and Malak said, 'I heard a bad word on the school bus today'?"

I started snickering and putting my head on her pillow, as if the memory might leak out, and I had to contain the thrill of it.

"Yes!" I whispered back. "Daddy's eyebrows went up, and he looked serious. We all glared at each other. He never swore. Ha-ha. He was, like, in first grade, right?"

Grace nodded and said, "And then Daddy asked him, 'What's the bad word, Malak?' He tried not to break a grin. Malak said, 'The F-word.'"

She and I melted into glorious, ceaseless giggles.

"And Daddy said, 'What word is that, Malak?' He was biting his lip, trying not to show a smirk. And Malak waited *forever* to answer, and then he said, 'Fish. I hate fish.'"

We burst into more laughter. "He is so funny, huh?" I said. "He was scared he was gonna get in trouble!"

"Yeah, Mommy. I miss him."

"Me, too, sweet baby. Me too."

Three months later, the official divorce day arrived. I invited Chad to the house. The court date was sandwiched between Grace's ninth birthday and the second anniversary of Malak's death, all in the first week of August.

When Chad came in the front door, he asked without skipping a beat, "What's up?"

I stammered as I examined his eyes, lips, and body language. "I … I don't know. I … I just … wanted to see you for a minute, I … guess."

I felt naked when he said, "You are looking for something different on my face, and you don't see it, do you?"

Wow. There it was. So obvious to him, but I felt like the girl who had slept with him for the first time. How had this guy, in all of his avoidance and distaste for me, who had run straight toward sometime "vile hatred" at the sight of me, *now* render a fast synopsis, accurately summing up my camouflaged invitation? *Darn. Coulda used that discernment for the past two years, darling.*

"You remember the note I wrote to the kids about you for their scrapbook?" I asked. "I almost forgot that I had written it. I made you a copy, even though I'm sure I read it to you a while back." I waived him to follow me upstairs to my bedroom. I handed him a copy.

"No." His voice sounded nervous. Sad.

"Oh." I smiled, with tears filling up my vision, "I wrote it ... before Malak died and everything ... else. I hope this means something to you."

His eyes melted. He glanced down. Once seated on the edge of the bed, he didn't move. At last, he whispered, "Oh ... thanks."

I hoped the letter I wrote the kids washed over him, somehow, with flashes of life in full color. I still believed in the man, in spite of our circumstance. I had not written in the scrapbook since before Malak died. Three-quarters of its pages, still empty.

"You can keep that copy," I offered.

His face reddened. "I'm sorry. I know I did the worst thing I could do to you."

I fumbled with my hands. It was like getting the one thing I always wanted and not knowing what to do when it arrives. I apologized to him, too. It must have been significant; he devoured my words as soon as they left my lips. I never told him about the affair with Ryan. Mostly, I feared more gossip but more, anger. We had made our decisions regardless. It changed nothing, and while Ryan and Caroline appeared to stay together, it protected the promise I made of secrecy to him. I protected his children. Silence protected Grace.

Chad had been the first to damage the marriage. In all the years I had been married to him, I never cheated until he refused to stop having the affair. It didn't make my actions right in any way, but I can sincerely say that Ryan and I would never have started anything, if not that the marriage vows had been violated a number of times already. I know that about myself. Yet the still small voice said to me, "You are not that impervious—clearly." But I had ended it. I had told him we could never be; it was finished. I had done the right thing. I don't believe that Chad or Caroline ever knew, until I told Chad, a decade later, for the sake of integrity and forgiveness. I told Grace too—I owed her that—but at that time, the gossip circus would have been more than I could take in Crazy Land. Maybe now, sanity could return.

A few hours after Chad left, I marched to the kitchen cupboard in pent-up frustration. Unable to achieve a sense of real anger release in a tangible way, I searched for a plate, a cup, or a piece of glass with potential. A coffee cup.

"Grace!"

"Yeah?" she said, walking into the kitchen. Grabbing her hand, I led through the front hall and out the front door to the base of the driveway at the street.

"What are we doing, Mama?"

"Do you ever get mad about Malak dying, or Mom and Dad's divorce, or just really feel mad and you can't seem to make it better?"

"Uh-huh." She squinched up her face.

"Oh, you are gonna love this! Yippee!" I snickered mischievously. Contrary to my stay-in-control nature, I felt deliciously derelict with juicy justification. A grand gesture in defiance of the cards I had been dealt. "Here. Take this." I put a mug in her hand. I held another mug in my other hand. I pulled my right arm back, preparing the force. "Throw like a man." I catapulted it to the ground, watching it scatter into tiny, feathery fragments. How very redemptive. "Your turn."

"No ... Mama," She slapped her leg, giggling.

"Yes! Come on—do it!" I doubled over in glee. She did it—we'd done it, laughing, half feeling guilty but warm inside. Emotions of failure and regret but "rightness" in the end had funneled through a simple coffee cup. *Mazel Tov*, *L'chaim*, and *Mahalo*!

"Uh-oh. Now we have to clean it up really well," I told her. "We don't want anyone to step on it and get hurt. Some of the fun just leaked out!"

Somewhere during the separation or divorce, Chad began dating Chelsea. I heard great things about her. They were rumored to be getting married. Grace spent every other week with them. She was having an instant blast with "new" brothers. I had the empty house. She was having *family* dinners. I was unemployed, so it was rice and beans—alone. *She* was going to the family farm, riding the family ATVs, and doing family tubing on the river. Chelsea was a great cook. She did scrapbooking with Grace. They had family movie night.

I never got to have any of this. Chelsea got the better part of the man that

I never had. Yeah. I felt jealous. Why did he never do that with us? I was happy for them, but as Grace came home to tell me all the fun they were having, it reflected my emptiness in contrast to his full life. As is typical in the transition of blended families, they loved each other and had their challenges too.

One night when Grace was staying with them, she called at midnight. "Mama, I'm not used to this house alone. Will you come and get me?"

Chelsea's boys and Grace were home alone. "No, but I will talk to you until you fall asleep, sweet pea."

"You will, Mama?"

"Sure, baby."

Three times she asked me if I had fallen asleep, but I promised her I was awake. I hung up after she did not answer, and I heard her breathing, the precious one. It was 1:00 a.m.

That small rift between Grace and Chad got bigger as Chad tried to make a strong relationship with Chelsea and the boys. In the course of a year, Grace craved time with her dad, and though he loved her very much, she became frustrated. Chad loved her the only way he knew how but maybe not in the way Grace needed. Chelsea was perfect for him. She hunted and fished, and she was pretty and intelligent. Grace and I both liked her.

Chelsea mentioned to Grace that Caroline and Ryan were getting a divorce. I was puzzled, because I still talked semi-regularly with Ryan, and he hadn't mentioned it. More exciting to Grace, her father promised to take her on a train trip, just the two of them. Shrieks of excitement filled the air. The day finally arrived, and Grace was floating. They took the train for a long weekend.

Flabbergasted at the thought that Ryan was divorcing and hadn't told me, I phoned his office, but it went straight to voicemail.

"Call me! I can't believe you didn't tell me. Are you happy, sad? What are you feeling?"

A couple hours, Ryan called back. "What are you talking about?" He blurted out.

"Eh, come on, Ryan! You know—the big news!" When he didn't respond, I said, "Your divorce, silly."

Had he hung up?

"Hello?" *I thought maybe we got disconnected.* "Oh no. Ryan? Did I say the wrong thing? Is it a secret?"

Pointedly, his voice came on the line. "If there *were* divorce papers being signed, I promise you, I would know about it."

Surely he was kidding around with me. This was a joke.

"Ah, are you sure she's not serving you papers, and you are the only one who doesn't know?" I proposed, joking and uncomfortable.

"We have talked about it," he admitted. "I have offered it up. She did not go for it. I have even pushed. So I am telling you. There are no papers being signed or negotiated currently in this house," Ryan finished.

"Wow."

After a brief silence, he queried, "Where did you hear this?"

Now for the double-whammy. This sucked. "Grace told me that Chelsea mentioned it. Chad had told her, which means only one thing. Caroline told Chad. They had a business meeting over Valentine's Day week." I then asked Ryan a hard question: "Is she wearing her wedding ring?"

"Yeah, yeah, she is," he replied confidently.

"I hate to say this, but I hear she's not wearing her ring during the day, and lots of people are noticing. No one really knows you from her work but me. No one else would be able to tell you this."

"Are you sure?"

"Sorry, but I'd bet my savings on it."

"Thanks." A soft exhale was heard from his end.

"I feel like the Devil, Ryan. I am so sorry to tell you this. But if you hadn't heard it from me, Grace might have told her friends, and it could have gotten back to your kids. I might have told mutual friends in the neighborhood. But I will tell Grace not to say anything, so nothing comes of it." We hung up.

When Chad returned with Grace, I called him. He was in a relationship with Chelsea. Caroline's lie was intentional and deceptive. Caroline likely removed her ring, purely for the sake of manipulation, to get Chad back. I don't even know if she wanted him in the end.

"Chad," I said. "I'm only telling you because the truth is important, and you have the right to make choices with all the information you are given. You decide what you want to do with this."

"Okay ..." his voice cautious, as if I was about to hit him with a baseball bat. I relayed the information I had gotten from Grace. He was not surprised by the divorce news. Then I told him what occurred when I called Ryan.

He was aghast. "Are you ... absolutely sure? Was he kidding with you?"

"On Malak's grave, Chad. If you had heard the silence on the other end of the phone when he heard me say divorce, I felt like the Devil. How horrible is it that someone else calls with that information? And what woman does that to the man she is still married to? When I asked him if she was her wearing a ring, Ryan said she wears it at home. Every night."

Quiet on the other end. Nothing. A breath, finally. "You are sure?"

"Yes. I thought you should know. It's none of my business, but if she is manipulating you, you have the right to an honest relationship, Chad. Make your decisions with all the information you have. I've always said you could marry her, if that makes you happy."

He was cold again. Short. He gave me nothing to read into over the phone.

We hung up.

I forgot about it. Things seemed fine. Later that day, he was supposed to see Grace, and he didn't call until late. He was a little angry, short, and said that the night had not gone as planned—he couldn't get Grace.

I received a phone call from Caroline.

"To what do I owe this surprise?" I asked with a laugh.

"Well ..." she said with diplomacy, "I heard you wanted to talk to me, so I was calling you."

With a deep breath, I laughed out loud, "Well, you've never known me to be silent, if I had something to say, Caroline. We already said it all. Is there some reason you want to talk? I'm open." I was curious, but I was in a good mood, and nothing was going to ruin it.

"That's funny," Caroline said, "because you sure have a lot to say lately about my life."

I split a rib. Tarred and feathered, the bird must be. "*Really. That's really funny*, Caroline. Because yes, I saw your best friends—Grace's softball coaches—all summer long and sat on the field with them. Chad had to coach with them. I never said *one* thing. I would have liked to, though. I saw my former hairdresser, who is also yours, *last night*, as a matter of fact. She asked me why I don't go to her anymore. I didn't want to blurt out that you were sleeping with my husband. And I could have. And yes, I have had plenty more opportunities when I've shut my mouth, only for your kid's sake and Ryan's, I promise you. What are we exactly talking about, Caroline?"

Then I got it. Chad had talked to her. I had spoken to Ryan, and she knew that too.

"You ... you are mad that I told your husband that you lied, aren't you? I am sorry." I couldn't believe this. I had a good laugh at her expense.

"Yes." Caroline said. "Whose business is it of *yours* to tell my business? You're not even married to him anymore." She only sounds mad about Chad, not Ryan, surprisingly.

"Really, that is rich, coming from the girl who wanted sloppy seconds from my husband. Wow, Caroline. I will likely speak to him forever, when it comes to Grace. For the record, I did not 'tattle' on you. My daughter told me, through Chelsea. So I honestly called your husband to tell him congrats—and the silence on the other end was *horrific*. Who does that to her husband, Caroline? I felt like the Devil, it was so mean. Are you kidding me? I would never hurt someone like that on purpose." Silence. When it was clear she wasn't going to respond, I went on. "Why would you ever do that to someone? For that matter, you should thank me. My daughter knows your daughter and her friends. What if your five-year-old runs up to Grace at school, and Grace says, 'Sorry to hear your parents are getting a divorce'? I just spared your girls more heartache than you ever did and ironically, undeniably more that you ever spared mine. You're welcome."

For the first time, she swallowed the lies equivalent to the size of a cat, and the silence was beyond glorious.

"You made this mess," I told her. "I fixed it for you before you hurt your own kids with it."

Caroline had lied, cheated, and betrayed me, but she tried to act as if *I* was in trouble?

Benevolence and justice. A nice combination.

"I don't have anything else, Caroline. I hope you have a great weekend. I wish you well. I have a fun night already planned. A date at the comedy club, so nothing is going to ruin it. I don't see a need to speak to you ever again."

"Yeah, you too." She mocked my laughter. Her voice was angry. That was our last conversation.

"Mom, I was just talking with an angel named Nadia, and she said that our miracles are coming this year," Grace said and then giggled.

Cheerily, I said "Oh, *really?*"

My worldview has changed to include errors and experiences that I would not have understood in the past. God is not limited to the box I put Him in. And Caroline is also His. I'm not proud of my behavior on many of these pages. It is embarrassing. But I am trying to live honestly. Who will find hope in the God of mercy and grace? Is there nothing more powerful than authentic Christianity and God's mercy?

CHAPTER 18

The Grave

I had tried to finish ordering Malak's gravestone and have it installed. Between money and Chad's excuses for not being available, it took five years. Five years. That's how lost we were. In the end, I told him I would pay for it and order it, and if he had anything to add, he better be there for the last meeting with the stone supplier.

He sighed on the phone. "I can't. I'm busy."

"Short of a natural disaster that kills you or the second coming of Christ, Chad, you ought to be there. But I will pay for it, order it, and get it done, with or without you, no excuses."

"You're right. You're right. Okay. I will meet you there."

We picked green marble (Malak's favorite color), and Chad decided to put a plethora of symbols on it (none of which I commented on)—a soccer ball, fishing poles, ducks, a deer, and a tree. I was amazed how he had an opinion when he hadn't said much for five years. He wasn't even going to come. When asked which one of us would be buried next to Malak, Chad burst out, "I am." That left me on the other side of the stone, by myself. I'd be facing away from Chad, which was fine, but it was like one last jab of the knife. I said nothing during the entire session. I just wrote out the check. I felt cold and was fighting to hide a face full of pain. I was left by Chad, erased and avoided for one final time. I shut the car door and cried on the steering wheel over the last of everything—the last thing that could hurt me, the last responsibility to Malak.

I have said to Chad some of the most horrible things I've ever said to anyone. I took most his transgressions very personally. I regret that. I didn't know better.

— CHAPTER 19 —

Monarch Butterflies

The phone rang.

It was my auntie Bea, who told me to write this down: "Suddenly, suddenly, suddenly. It will be extraordinary. Extraordinary. You will *know* that it is God, more than at any other time in your life." I thanked her, we prayed together and ended the call.

In making decisions for my daughter, I was never certain what choices were the right ones. I had just been earnestly praying about my future, moments before she called. I needed that kind of a precise word of confidence. I was unemployed, and my industry was dying out in our small town. I had turned down jobs I didn't want in hope of something better. I wished I could leave, but ... not with Chad here, but I told no one. Grace, though, was hinting that she wanted to move away.

"Hi, Mom."

"Honey, I've been praying for you, and something extraordinary is coming for you. I know it."

"Did you speak to Auntie Bea?" I queried.

"No." she said.

"She told me the same thing, yesterday! Hm. That's weird." I laughed.

"I have to go, I just called to tell you that. I love you." She replied.

"Okay, thanks. Love you."

Curious about their choice of *extraordinary*, I decided to look up the definition of it and found that it means, 1) going beyond what is usual, regular, or customary; 2) exceptional or remarkable; or 3) sent for or employed by a special function or for special service or occasion. As an ambassador of the extraordinary or minister extraordinaire.

I had to think about definition number three for a while.

I wrote the definition on a crumpled piece of paper. Over six months, I moved that paper from my purse, to my pocket, to my makeup bag, to a drawer. I kept it. Evidence of a promise to me. I had asked God for something abnormally extravagant and visibly significant to the greatest of critics, as ransom for Malak's death and payment for all that was seemingly wasted of our histories. A promise, from so unlikely a place—*a dictionary.* The substance of things hoped for and the evidence of things not seen. God whispered back. *Go, baby. Go.*

I am commissioned for a purpose as an ambassador of the extraordinary, employed/sent by God for a special purpose. A minister of sorts. Under a King's authority. An ambassador of the extraordinary, I was appointed by the King to sign and make decisions on behalf of the King in His absence. Not something I chose. It was something so big as to be nonrepeatable and profitable.

"Mom, I'm kidding about the Nadia part," Grace confessed, "but I really think miracles are coming this year. I think Dad's gonna marry Chelsea. That will make me happy. We will move to California. I had a dream that you married a dark-haired, dark-skinned man and you will get your dream job, your best ever. You'll even get to travel."

She said she pictured a view of the ocean from a cliff in a city that looked like Greece. Her Dad and Chelsea were on the veranda of an exquisite home near us. Our family was waving to them from our cliff-side outdoor patio. I was on my way to work on a film, and she was in college. "Mama, your cup is overflowing. You won't know what to do, but even though you feel like you're going to choke on your blessings, gulp it down, Mom. Even though it keeps on coming. And we will give God all the credit!" Sleepily, she whispered, "The storm is over, The sun is coming out. Winter's almost over, and summer is coming."

I sat up. I turned on the light and grabbed a pen and paper from the nightstand and wrote it all down. I absolutely believed it. Out of the mouths of babes.

She was right.

Chad married Chelsea two months later. Chelsea's first husband had died, leaving her to raise two boys. Funny that Chad lost one son but is blessed with two boys to love with an open heart. I believe that what one person was not able to do, another person is able to accomplish. Chelsea had been praying for a dad for her two sons for nine years. Having seen the father's photo on the walls, all that they had lost became obvious. How could I not want the riches of life back to a woman who just wanted happiness again?

When they came to pick up Grace, I wished them well, though we all stared at the floor in discomfort and emotion. I bit my lip to fight off tears both of hurt and happiness. I reached through the car door window and hugged Chelsea. Woman to woman, we understood each other. I had tried to bless them, in my own way.

Sure, I was a little frustrated that Chad was already getting his life back in perfect form—family and wife.

Grace and I prayed for Chad and Chelsea.

A few short weeks passed.

"Mom, I think we should move. Let's just leave on an adventure. California sounds fun."

"Why California, Grace? Having all of our family in Illinois, why would we move there?"

"You told me that if you ever moved, it would be to California one time."

"But Grace, you don't know anything about it. I wouldn't do that 'til after you graduated. You can't leave the state anyway, as part of the divorce."

"I just wanna go."

I smiled at her. "Did you know that I was born there?"

"You *were*?"

"Yeah, sure. In a perfect world that might be fun, but you have a life here with your dad. No more California talk, Grace."

Over the course of more than a year, Grace hinted, implied, suggested, and dreamed of moving to the land of sun and sand. California. She hounded me almost daily. Three kids came to speak at her school, and they were from California. She said it was a sign. *She's all of eleven years old. I forbid it*, in the beginning.

The conversations became obsessive for Grace. I yelled at her for such persistence. On one such occasion, I put my finger in her face and told her to stop the discussion. The divorce decree forbade our leaving the state.

Stomping off, I left her crying in the car in the complete darkness of the garage. I slammed doors leading to my bedroom. I turned on the TV in frustration of her pushy pursuits, and one of my favorite pastors was preaching. I don't remember his exact words, but it went something like this:

"Sometimes, you are pregnant with something no one else understands. Like Mary and Elizabeth. They shared a baby/birthing experience in the tummy. A vision. One knew and understood the other's purpose and dreams. Sometimes you are about to give birth to something no one else can see or understand. They don't even get it. You carry it for nine months in the dark, not able to see the secret/vision inside you, but you feel it."

Wow. Here I was, condemning Grace for a vision she didn't understand but I secretly dreamed of. I broke into waterworks. Grace was pushing this move to LA, not ever having set foot there. It was against everything that made sense, even to me. I ran to the car to get her. She was still in the car, her eyes swollen. "Come here," I said, grabbing her hand.

"What?" she asked.

"You gotta see this!"

When we entered my room, there was a Scripture verse on the TV, written over the whole screen: "Ask in my name, whatever you will, and believe, and it shall be given to you."

Hugging, we apologized. She had a blessing in her for both of us. She admitted that she didn't understand it, but I realized I had to guard the gift in my little girl. Don't speak against your blessing.

Interestingly, not long after that, my mom visited us from the Carolinas. Mom was seated on the couch. She glanced out the front window. Southern Illinois terrain is green and very flat in the summer. Her brow lifted, but without a word, she looked in the other direction. I stared out the front window. *It would be so nice to live near the ocean*, I thought. *I'm going to live near the ocean one day.*

Mom was still quiet on the couch. Knowing her like I do, I asked her what the expression on her face meant. Matter-of-factly, she said, "I think you're going to live by the ocean." What had made her think that? She didn't know. It was something about the sky in the window. What if I had ignored my inclination to ask her that question? Sometimes, I believe it's as if she is speaking our lives into existence. Something good was coming.

Later that night, we were praying for Chad and Caroline when Mom stopped in the middle to explain. "I think I just saw you married while we were just praying. He has dark hair and skin. I did not see his eyes. He has two children."

No, my family doesn't usually see visions.

My mom had lived in California when she was eighteen years old. I was born there. I was raised in Chicago, however, and went to college in Chicago for two years. Then I transferred to California in my junior year, though I never understood my own fascination. I mentioned the comedy of it all to my dad on the phone. Dad regaled me with a little anecdote about the monarch butterfly. He told me that monarch butterflies will return to the birthplace of their parents, having never been there prior. The evening news had just done a piece on precisely this. I found that fascinating. The very next morning, Grace called me from school. She had forgotten her science project at home. Could I bring it to school as soon as possible?

"What is it?" I sighed, annoyed.

Grace said excitedly, "It's the caterpillar in the jar in my room. I hope it doesn't die today, because it turned into a butterfly last night, and it looked like it wasn't doing so well."

Another unmistakable golden thread. I had a clear sense that we would be moving to California now, but without Chad's consent, it would be impossible. I would never ask that of him. We had been through enough.

Grace mentioned moving to her father. As expected, he was mad, not to mention hurt. He had every right to be. Hadn't he suffered enough punishment already in his life? Grace and Chad had a history of their own. They had fences to mend. They fought for months—her anger over his affair. Her fury and rejection because they didn't spend one-on-one time alone. After counseling appointments and, according to Grace, failed attempts to spend more time with him, she wanted to leave.

The final conversation was painful.

"Grace, you are selfish for wanting to leave," he told her.

"Dad, you are selfish for leaving us. You have been the selfish one. You don't spend time with me, and I don't think it's going to change. Just let me go."

Maybe Chad knew this about himself, deep down.

A short time after that, Chad called me. "Go ahead and take her." Resignation was in his voice.

"I'm sorry—what?"

"Move. It's fine."

Okay ... thanks." I felt sad and unsure if I should do it, even if I could. There was no reason to stay. My parents didn't live here; there was no family in this town. A new start sounded so very wonderful.

I think Chad surrendered to letting her go at the risk of losing her to her anger if he didn't. Chad realized his mistakes and was paying a heavy price for all that had happened. Too much, really. He was beaten down. There was no court case. No arguments. It was like getting the keys to a free life for both of us. We were free from small-town scrutiny, gossip, and the Johnson family. No more driving by the accident site. Chelsea didn't have the ex-wife to deal with and neither did Chad. There were some advantages. It took me all day to grasp the miracle. I could find employment. A new path to blaze. I went out first, scouting apartments.

The morning that Grace was moving to Los Angeles to live with me, she called while packing for her flight.

"Mom, I was so scared, wondering if I was doing the right thing. I feel terrible, leaving my dad. I've been trying not to lose it. How can I do this? But I found a penny on my windowsill this morning in my room at Dad's house. I found two pennies on the closet floor. One penny in my suitcase ..." She trailed off into sniffles. "And another one in the laundry basket."

"Aw, sweet pea. My heart hurts for you. It's gotta suck. I'm sorry this is where life is now. You can stay there, or move back at any time. I will buy the ticket tomorrow if you want."

Looking at apartments, we scouted a cute studio-sized, newly renovated location. I had been there twice before, doing research. I brought Grace with me for her approval. She liked it immediately. After walking through it, we stopped in the center of the barren room of white walls and chocolate hardwood floors. Grace glanced down.

"Look, Mom."

"Huh?" I answered, somewhat distracted.

"A penny."

At our feet, a single penny lay on the floor between us.

"This is the place then!" I said.

From four thousand square feet to a one-bedroom apartment. No yard or back patio. No neighborhood BBQs. No washer and dryer. No suburban neighborhood. I could hear the neighbors talking. And the footsteps of the tenants upstairs. The wind whispered through the older walls. No triple garage or security system. Street parking permits were required. Palm trees and blue sky every single day. No fireplace, no snow. There was graffiti, homelessness, vast religious and cultural diversity, and rude drivers with horrific traffic. I did not want to be anywhere else. Pinch me.

The day our furniture arrived, Grace unpacked one of our most prized possessions. It was a garden sculpture—an angel, resting peacefully on a traditional Greek column, a dark wood pedestal. We unwrapped it carefully, and it was the crowning adornment to our little sanctuary. Both of us sighed, as if the masterpiece had arrived. It felt like home now. In her sweet, soft-spoken, other-worldly-inspired way, my Grace said of the statue representing my angel in heaven, "Look, Mama. See how his hand is casting miracles in the room. It's like he's spreading them all around us."

My heart stopped. "It does."

How did she come up with these descriptive, rich phrases, so beyond her years? They were words with wings, taking me to dimensions I hadn't considered. It was a plumb line of the promises past and promises future.

I dropped Grace off at her first day of school. I headed to the DMV for California plates. I took a seat next to a pretty, curvy African American woman. I was dressed up for an interview.

She smiled politely. "I hope it goes quick, because I have to be somewhere."

"Me too," I responded.

"You look so nice today," she added.

"Oh, thank you, sweet woman. I've had the suit a long time."

"What kinda car you drive? You drive a Mercedes?"

"Oh, no. That would be fun, but I have a VW Jetta. You?"

"Oh, my girlfriend won the lottery and bought me a used Mercedes," she admitted.

"How nice of her! That's so exciting. Dang, we all need friends like that, huh?"

We laughed some more.

"You must have a great job though, right?" she asked.

"Actually ..." I sighed. "No."

"Oh. You look like you're—"

"Let me give you the two-sentence story of my life. I haven't worked in three years, my son died in a car accident and I was the driver, and my husband and I got a divorce after he had an affair with my former BFF. If my parents hadn't helped me, I ..." I broke the tension with snickers. "I guess maybe it appears that my life is together on the outside, but it's definitely not."

"That's messed up," she said. "I'm sorry."

"You know, you can handle anything if you keep your faith. I'm sure you have your own story. What do you do for work?"

"I work at a bank. I guess it's okay." She patted her dress, looking down. A gold cross was around her neck.

"What would your dream job be, if you could do anything?" I asked her.

"I would be an opera singer. I used to sing more."

"Hey, I love singing too! You need to do that more often."

"Yeah," she agreed.

"Can I pray for you?" I asked shyly.

She nodded. "I would like that."

"Dear Lord Jesus, I don't know what the plan for this woman's life is, but bless her beyond anything she ever imagined. Use her voice, and surprise her with how you will use her. Connect her for the opera with divine favor. Please speak loudly to her about what and where she should go to find her financial blessings and her purpose. Give her houses she didn't build, and restore the years the moths have eaten. Give her specific wisdom to protect her and grant her a special man who helps her finish her purposes on this earth. Bring her courage and strength and bold confidence. Change her life radically, Lord. In Jesus' name, amen."

She cried, sitting there in the DMV, and thanked me. "I haven't had anyone pray for me like that in a long time."

I remember thinking how nice it was to encourage someone else in such an odd circumstance. Her perception of me was that of a privileged, polished woman, but we shared messed-up lives and faith under the skin. I never see myself the way she did. People's perceptions of us are rarely accurate whether good or bad.

"Bacardi, diet, with a lime, please." I gestured to the bartender. In my silver pointy heels and a tailored slit-skirt suit, I hung my briefcase under the bar. Door after door had closed in my face that day. I wanted a solid sales job. A dark and gorgeously well-dressed Italian piece of deliciousness sat next to me and introduced himself. At first, it seemed he wanted a little rendezvous. He threw out his European bravado and innuendo. He expressed interest in helping me with my career. His fascinating stories of working with celebrities and criminals stole my attention. In the interest of killing the mood of passion and creating a conversation of substance, I told him my story. My faith. He revealed his desperate desire to have children with his wife of many years, but she was unable to conceive. It was killing them both. They appeared to be on their last thin golden thread.

It was as if my hand moved on its own. He told me of the rich religious history of his family for hundreds of years. His was a prominent heritage in their country of defending the government and in international business. I felt compelled to tell him something.

"The Lord has such tremendous things for you. You need to walk in that blessing. You have an incredible purpose. Huge. Don't slack off now. You have huge things to do that you haven't considered. You are extremely influential. Keep your faith. Walk in your calling. Boldly. You have no idea." Inexplicably, my palm reached toward his forehead with a gentle push. I couldn't help myself. I had to contact him on the forehead. More incredulous, he leaned into my hand, and I pushed back. "Don't you see it?" I asked. I can't tell you why, but I had do and say all that.

He nodded knowingly. In my own head, I thought, *How disrespectful? Why did I just do that to an acquaintance?* I would normally *never* do that.

At the end of our conversation, I asked if I could pray for him. He agreed. I don't remember everything I said, but he responded with "wow" and "amen." All the way home, I could not stop praying for him. What an interesting man. What a candid conversation for two strangers. I'll call him "Romeo."

One year later, I called Romeo for a lawyer referral off of his business card. With soft intensity to his voice, he said, "Thank you for your prayers. I have to tell you, I have a perfect little baby girl, now two months old. Two weeks after you prayed, my wife was pregnant! Thank you."

I began to sniffle in awe of God.

Had I not called that man for the referral, I would have never known the answered prayers. What if I had never met that man, heard his broken heart, or prayed? God is amazing. I believe I'm gifted to pray for children, out of my experience. This was the first evidence of that.

Feeling so grateful for my new life, I sent Chad an e-mail, spilling my thanks and remorse to my ex-husband. We had said one day that we would cry over all that was lost, together, since our happier days. I felt so full of love for him. I always will. He gave me a chance at a life, regardless of what it cost him. He paid so dearly in life's depravity, giving up Grace in the end. All the people who judged us and got angry *with* us because of our departure to Los Angeles didn't walk in his shoes. His is a higher caliber of man. A lesser man would have selfishly protected the right to be her father in righteous indignation. Actually, I would be the first to defend that right *for* him. The better man that he is, he knows he is her father, by right and by privilege both. She loves him. She is part of him. Grace has a journey to find. Nothing will separate them, certainly not distance. Even if we lived three miles away, they had some valleys to travel. Questions to ask. Grace to walk. Anger to flush.

I asked Chad's forgiveness for my anger and blame, for the temper I had when we were married under all that difficulty, for all that he had taught me about love, and my strengths and maybe more poignantly, my weaknesses. A family can teach you best about your shortcomings. I argue that your in-law family teaches you most about your own family. We traded conversations about our families that aided our perspective on things—for the better, mostly. I thanked him for a multitude of precious memories and a fantastic life. For a gorgeous son and a once rare and uncommonly happy marriage. At least, for me. For the grace it took to be my man and the way he made me proud in so many capacities as his wife. For the grand-scale forgiveness it took to forgive me my fatal blow that demolished all of our lives and the peace and happiness we once had. For all the condemning words I had ever spoken that had ever hurt him and that, I pray, linger no longer. I love him. I always will. I don't regret marrying him at all. I don't know if there was anything more I could have done. I tried believing and encouraging him, but when you don't love yourself, you don't make good choices and that affects others.

But I write it, not as a woman who is in anyway lamenting the past...but in a forward moving, healing, love carved and heart-washing, finger-painted letter of gratitude in all things. It took me years to get to this peace, but nothing feels better than letting go in love. Accepting the beauty for my ashes. One of my life's greatest gifts came from the man whose name means "battle warrior." From that severed relationship, I owe tremendous gratitude for the life I now have. His impact on my life is one of the most generous, forgiving, and rewarding assets of who I am as a person, aside from my parents, and Grace, of my lifetime thus far. Truthfully. How could I not honor the man who lived through this with me?

I will strive to exemplify love, mercy, and character for the rest of my life. Everything else is irrelevant. In that order.

— CHAPTER 20 —

Nothing, Nothing, Nothing Is Impossible, So Believe

Ten years have passed since Malak's death. This chapter is a collection of stories and funny happenings that are part of the golden threads:

Living in Los Angeles, California, I'm still a single mom. Still fall asleep with my Bible on the empty side of the bed. A great story I must tell you. I called a cleaning company to get my couches and an area rug cleaned. When the two workers arrived, they found me vacuuming under the cushions of the couch and chair. I found pennies and lint, feathers, and crumbs.

"All right, gentleman, have at it!"

As they started to move the furniture, I noticed the two men looking at each other with a funny expression.

"Is everything okay?" I asked.

"Here," one man said as he handed me a pair of Hanes white briefs.

I was perplexed. I walked over to Grace, who was on the computer. "So, can you think of any reason why this pair of boys underwear was in the couch?"

"No," Grace answered nervously, in an attempt to avoid any trouble that she wasn't guilty of.

"Grace, did a boy from your high school leave them here?"

"I ... no. I don't know." She seemed completely surprised, too.

Perfectly folded, like they were freshly washed, I began unfolding them to examine them closer. "How did they—" My eyes fell on the size of the underwear. "Oh my."

Grace's face went pale.

"Do you know what these are? These are Malak's. Hanes, boys size eight. Just the size an eight-year-old boy wears. He died when he was eight."

"Where did you find these? I have had this furniture for ten years. I have personally moved it four times, removing the cushions myself, and I have cleaned them. Where did you find them?" I practically begged the men for an answer, so perplexed was I.

"You'd have never found them, ma'am. They were folded just the right size to fit between the lining and underneath the curved arm of the chair."

I laughed when I remembered how Malak put M&M's in the recliner, and I would find Pop-Tarts under chairs in the family room near the TV. I'd bought the furniture ten years ago. Malak died nine years ago. Somehow, a clean, folded pair of underwear made its way to a hiding spot in a chair that had been saved for this day for us to find. Nine years later. Fifteen hundred miles across the country. Four moves. It was another golden thread that made me smile. You can't make this up.

Does life really come full circle? Pain becomes joy with people and places I never would have imagined in my future. The destiny that only Malak's death brought forward. Now miracles, healing, and promise erupted out of life's forfeitures. Finally, there was freedom, joy, and a feeling of fitting into a plan bigger than myself. I have begged God with everything I am not to waste the experiences. God cares enough to prove His purpose in all of us in our journeys of fatal mistakes. And how much He loves us.

It reminds me of something, long forgotten, that happened when Malak was three years old, I was sitting on his beach pail in the middle of the basement floor, crying and praying over my lost sense of purpose between dishes and diapers. Many a mom wonders if she has the greatest job, simply taking care of her children, but wonders, too if that is enough, for her life's purpose. Is there more? And if your loved one dies, what purpose can you find? Like a voice in the past whispering in my memory, suddenly I remembered a conversation with my little man. As if God was encouraging through Malak's words, from a time before he died. While I was crying, Malak put one small hand on my shoulder with his chubby perfect fingers, and pushed my hair off my face with the other hand. He got his nose in front of mine, and with a sad smile and looking at me through those long eyelashes, he said in a singsong voice, "Don't cry, Mommy. Your daddy knows your tears." Those words floated in on a satin blanket and lingered in the atmosphere, and they comfort me even now. Golden, beautiful woven threads. What made a three year old think, to tell me my father's thoughts, but the mind of God, Himself?

For eighteen months prior to Malak's death, I was reading Scriptures—randomly, it would seem. But suddenly, they made more sense. Foretold to me in love, speaking through my childhood Bible, God was telling me of things to come. I frequently landed on the biblical phrase "the fatherless and the widow." Five times in one day. Foreshadowing. Chad and I would become one father/mother to one less child and the term "widow" means long-term separation from a spouse, not just in death. "Malak" (meaning "messenger") is unavoidably symbolic. In a way, Malak liberated me to another life. I was victorious in overcoming my circumstance. God's message to me about my life's purpose came through my son, which has become my purpose to others.

On the eve of Yom Kippur, I decided to drive two and a half hours to hear a preacher speak. I was desperate to hear from God, if I had to choke him somehow. I was feeling lost yet again. The preacher's sermon went well, but I pondered my obedience and whether God would meet me here.

Walking up to the preacher, I said, "Thank you for speaking tonight. I wondered if you would pray for me."

"Ah. He saved the best for last," he said with a smile. "What's your story?"

"I lost a son. I'm fine. It's been many years, but I need a specific word of direction, actually."

His face looked pained. He paused and then said, "What was your son's name?"

"Malak." And as is typical of me, I didn't wait for his response before telling him the meaning of that name.

He shook his head.

"What?" I asked.

"Malak. That is *so* speaking to me."

"What do you mean?"

"In Isaiah 6, I'm thinking of you. The angel touches the lips of Isaiah and says, 'Your iniquity and guilt are taken away and your sin is completely forgiven you.'"

"Oh, yeah," I said softly.

"You should read that chapter," he added. The preacher looked far away for a moment, and then the familiar sadness surfaced on his face. "I had a young son that died, too."

"How long ago?"

"I ..." After a long pause, he said, "I can't."

"It's okay. I understand." I had unwittingly caused him pain, so much so that it was obvious. He had no idea of the time frame. "You know, God won't waste this. I have asked God to raise a child from the dead for someone else, to save marriages, and heal sick children. Who knows how you might use this?" I said.

Quiet.

"Don't let this take you down," I urged him. "Press God for something miraculous. Press God for a promise of redemption somehow. Be a great man of wisdom and healing so that *nothing* of you or *Him* is wasted."

"Can you do something for me?" he asked. "I rarely do this? Will you pray for me?"

I smiled. "Of course."

I came needy. I left full. I went to bless someone else instead of myself, as it turned out.

We prayed, and as I finished, he said, "I think you're going to help millions of people. Thank you."

In Isaiah 6, the Lord asks, "Whom shall I send?" and Isaiah responds with

"Here am I. Lord, send me." The Lord said, "Go and tell this people."

I knew my call. I knew my "crazy" had a purpose. I knew my God had heard me in my aimlessness. I believed. For another day.

Scripture warns us to choose a name carefully. I had no idea how pivotal or significant Malak would become. Grace ("favor, blessing") led the way on the path of this journey with great destiny.

I never imagined the importance of the golden threads along the way in our lives, and I reflected on their substance and meaning, starting with my scrapbook love letter to the kids and to Chad that turned out to be the last one—now a remnant, more important than in the moment it was written. Then there was the original prayer to conceive Malak, (then appearing medically impossible) but now quite ironic. Malak's vision of a demon. Malak's wearing his seatbelt, but that being the instrument that killed him. Malak's drawing of the endangered cars. The pennies that bear the words "In God We Trust" and "Liberty." Heads up—"change" is coming. Malak's penny loafers finally falling off the bed, months later, as if the shoe knew I was waiting for the other shoe to drop. Malak's premonition of death. His curiosity ride to a graveyard a month before he died. My losing my job and turning down jobs with twice my salary just before Malak died, so that I could enjoy one eternally significant summer. The monarch butterfly story, and Grace's caterpillar turning into a butterfly on the same day I heard it, seeming to confirm a move to California. Finding several pennies the day Grace left Chicago. Moving to the "Miracle Mile" district in Los Angeles. The penny on the apartment floor. The underwear in the chair. While these coincidences and golden threads connect us to God and each other, I like to think they nudge us in the right direction and strengthen our resolve to take another step forward toward destiny and purpose that God has for our lives.

I was hearing the term "perfect storm" repeatedly in my head for a few weeks recently. Every time I thought of it, I decided to speak a confession from my lips.

"I am in a perfect storm. A whirlwind of God's blessing and favor are on my life. Everything that isn't a blessing will be gone when the storm hits. The only remaining pieces will be my blessings. I'm getting a husband. I'm getting my finances back. I'm getting my career launched. All in the perfect storm. A storm of restoration. A storm of redemption. A favor and glory storm." If life can drop losses in thirty seconds, why can't God restore it the same way?

This went on for a week.

Driving to work at the end of the week, I turned on the radio. The first thing the DJ said was, "The *Andrea Gail* left the port off the East Coast in 1991. She never returned. The perfect storm was the biggest storm in US history. All that remained of the ship was a few small fragments. There were three components to the storm: a nor'easter from Canada; a warm front off of New York; and Hurricane Grace had just swept over the area." Not hurricane Judy or Rubin or Sally—Hurricane *Grace*. It made me think of the ten years that followed Malak's death and the grace of God it took to thrive after that hurricane that devastated my life. Compelled to pull over, I then grabbed my phone and Googled "the *Andrea Gail*."

The perfect storm was a Halloween nor'easter. The storm lasted from

October 28 to November 2. It was an October day, that day, and the original name of the Andrea Gail was *Miss Penny*.

I laughed out loud. "God, you are funny."

Another golden thread on the road to the perfect storm of redemption and blessing.

I do, however, ponder *some* questions. Such as, why does someone survive a plane crash and another suddenly die of an impossibly small ant bite? Why is there a miracle on one corner and a monstrosity across the street?

I inconceivably missed the primary point of the film, *The Passion of the Christ*. I got sidetracked on a secondary point, as I related to the mother, Mary, and did not grasp God's love for me but His love for His Son. Watching Mary's loss as Jesus died on the cross was excruciating. Most people find a King, beaten senselessly and rejected, but I was bruised with Mary, whose child died to save the whole world. What then, did Malak really die for? Mary *knew* why Jesus died. These are just the honest questions with which I have to make peace. Christ died to save the whole world. The more time passes, the more I recognize how the life I experience shapes who I have become. I can't be sorry for who I have become, however I got here. To you, as a reader, despise not your trials. What if they are pivotal to your purpose?

I'll make another selfish observation, and I am sure I am not alone in this perspective: regularly we have heard the story of Abraham, who walked his son Isaac up the hill toward the altar, where he obediently raised a blade to kill his son. Yet how perfectly God interrupted with another sacrifice of a lamb in the thicket, which spared his son at the last minute.

Every time I hear that passage I dare say to God in my heart, "But you saved Isaac. You didn't save Malak. What is the lesson of unanswered prayer? I raised the blade, I killed the boy, and You *didn't* save him." The sermon is always preached that God is never too late to save. God was late, on that day. My conclusion is that one day, I will see the graciousness of God in my unanswered prayers play out beautifully, not just in heaven but also in my life. Maybe more gorgeously in Grace's.

If this story offers answers to questions about God, faith, or how to overcome a challenge, fantastic. If one person falls softly to his or her knees and identifies with the words of hope and rescue in damaged circumstance, then hallelujah! If these words walk others through angry paces, or they identify with my tirades and honest admissions, you've met me, and I hope to encourage you onward.

A wise man once told me, "It doesn't matter what the offense. Forgiveness is a long and equal distance across a canyon, either way." There are six degrees of separation between us all. I stand shoulder-to-shoulder in the eyes of heaven with every other sinner made a saint by grace. Including Chad and Caroline. No matter the offense. We don't perfect ourselves first and then run into church for acceptance. No, we run bleeding, deranged, and madly unrecognizable.

Forgiveness. Sometimes we want someone to blame. Even the noblest people will have such a proclivity. If I just beat myself up for my mistakes for some contrived amount of time, I am redeemed from it. This is not just illogical but also impractical and contrary to the gift of forgiveness in the foundations of faith. I am no surprise to God. I need healing, and God is the creative one who can see my wounded gaps and knows just how to kiss over them in His kindness, regardless of the malfeasance. I was never elected to carry the scepter of forgiveness for reparation on whomever *I* deemed *worthy*. No, God does the judging. Sin gets me to the cross faster. Who am I, but in Christ alone?

Since the accident, I have gained insights but also an anointing to pray for marriages, infidelity, children, and barren women. I have noticed a new gift for discernment to pray for people.

For example, there was one couple in church whom I admired from a distance. The husband, a highly recognized, world-traveled professional in his field and his wife, gorgeous and quite accomplished in her own right. We do not know each other. Randomly, I prayed for their marriage and the health of their children. I started seeing them everywhere. Him alone. Her alone. Two of them on a date. I felt like a stalker. How weird. At one point after a few months of sitting in the pew, I saw a scant space between heads in the rows. There they were, all the way across—again! They couldn't see me, but I smiled. *What, Lord? What do you want?* I must be nuts. I had been praying for their marriage, yet they appear blissful. Why?

As I slid back in the church pew, perturbed, my hand caught on something tight in the crack between the backrest and the seat cushion. I pulled it out. A wedding band. Gold and busted in a perfect half circle. Broken marriage vows? I didn't know for sure. And who had left it there? What of that person's pain? Was it a token offering of someone's hidden bitterness or shame? Or did the person even know it was lost there? What became of *that* person's secret?

Big gulp. Big exhale. *God? I'll keep praying.*

Believe in a golden thread. A thread of faith. Steady and strong. It finds you signing your name on the divorce documents and death certificates. When heaven meets you with your car running in a closed garage, pondering your own demise. God responds to you in the simple things, too—when the sun shines on your face, and you had long forgotten what good ice cream tasted like. The golden thread sustains you, when you dare shake an angry fist at the seemingly arrogant, careless sky.

Standing atop a Bible maybe with a middle finger cursing my losses and my Savior. His grace loved me still. Knew my pain. Claiming that I still believe with all my might, though I'd rather curse the life and the God who gave it, when in my hour of betrayal. In the noisy insanity, *he* kept *me*. We will be tested like Job and in grave error like King David; *and still* pursue God nonetheless relentlessly.

Whether you are in a church pew next to me, or written to that reader whose own unimaginable secrets afflict them, this letter is to you; it also is to someone who won't set foot in a perceived "hypocritical" church. We are all hypocritical at some point. We have opinions. We don't always live up to them. My walking-disaster story was told for your benefit. It was a story that blessed me eventually and saved me, bringing me from pointlessness to purpose. I am the lost soul with huge needs on any given day, and I seek to fix them. When left to my own devices, I would choose skinny menthol cigarettes, Bacardi, swearing, and a cute guy. Just put on more lipstick and eyeliner, tease my hair, lift my chin, and pretend I'm handling it. Dress and cover up the hot mess.

But now I am less inclined to grab for such compulsions, since I know who's holding my hand. I don't have it all together, but I am wholly loved by God. In disaster, we are captive to an impossible situation that requires a defiant "rise" out of us in order to thrive.

Stand up and take victory. Steal, no, *take* your life back. Fight for the future you want. Love limitlessly and unselfishly. We can't purchase a six-pack of integrity or a pill for perseverance. Stare down your obstacles. Whatever your weakness, hidden secret, or public catastrophe, embrace it, reconcile it, pray over it. *Conquer* it. If God is *for* you, who can be against you? I would suggest that you harness your challenge. You will find it is designed to bless you with your own gift in disguise. You are equipped to do something amazing with your life—something mind-blowing, if you dare. *You.* It is intended for your golden threads and *your* tapestry. It is far less random than it is perceived to be; you need only listen for your purpose.

Your story matters. You have one life. Do something good with it. Love fat and sassy. Laugh louder. Kiss more often. Wiggle your silly toes in the sand. Be drunk with joy. Wallow in peace. Sing off key. Be drenched in gratitude. Drown in faith.

CHAPTER 21

What's the Answer?

Struggling with how exactly to get the point across, you likely will find your purpose in your greatest pain. This book is really the story of God's grace and mercy on my life. Period.

What are you left with? Should there be a list of steps? Some people want that answer. Should it be the perfect ending to my life, as if redemption swept in and the miraculous occurred? Hm. Can't really give you that.

Do you dare admit that you felt as though God was not only late but that He let you down? This book is for when God said no and things went very different from what you planned. This story is for all the people who felt as though God did not step in and save the day. What then? Things happen that make you question the predictability of the future, question your ability to love freely, and to trust that everything will be okay.

Maybe you got what you needed in the questions that were wrestled over—the infusion of strength that comes in a belief in God. Those of you who might consider going to church or watching a faith broadcast, may you find encouragement, stability and answers, even.

Life is murky. The waters are gray in this story. But God is not. He has a plan, even in the worst times. If this story sparks action in some way, to be compelled to pray, then, amen!

Striving ferociously to make life complete, to build a life that remotely resembles what I remember before Malak's death, is a bit like chasing clouds. That image makes me smile. Are you chasing clouds, trying to wrap your arms around something elusive? I think all of us have fond memories of the past—happier, full of love and laughter. Those times, however, often were not as we remember. I hate to admit that I have held that part of my life in high regard by comparison. It represents a season of solidness, before trauma. Being married and in love, I was more relaxed on the weekends. We had a real yard, and BBQs, vacations, comfortable bank accounts, and I enjoyed being "in the moment." I acknowledge that I have spent a decade attempting to make it up to Grace in some way. Trying to get something back. Unfortunately, that will never return. Not that I wanted Chad. Or Chicago winters. I just wanted the best new life I could find, as fast as possible. It is exhausting to claw out of a dirt hole, but the minute I reach the top, the ground crumbles, and I slide down again. And yet, I feel as if God shifted something inside me, finally. Hallelujah—it took ten years to find "contentment".

Quit trying to fix this life in every way possible and wearing yourself out. I've really enjoyed my life as it is. Don't miss a decade trying to get to some undefined place that makes you "satisfied." Life has already become quite, perfect—this hour of this day. It took too long for me to let go of my expectations on redemption. A relationship with Jesus. That's redemption.

God is as powerful as ever in our midst. Fear is as ever present, as always. But God does have a beautiful plan for our lives, one that makes us surrendered servants—bold, faith-speaking, effective people for the purpose of God. Dynamic encouragers. Relentless pursuers after Jesus. Vessels for the audacious. Believers in miracles. When it's really bad on the horizon, the funny thing is, we stop asking God to fix things or do this or that, and we ask God to be personal to us—five minutes at a time. We want Him to be so intimate with us, merely so that we can just make it through the day. That is all we really need on any day of any year in any life.

After pondering and perusing, I have decided that I trust Him—carte blanche. Though He slays me, yet will I trust Him. These are the snarly, derailing but not uncommon life experiences we face, where the strength of our character is constructed expertly. Where miracles could be born of obliterated existence. Where God could teach us His own unfathomable creativity for our lives.

There is passion where numbness sought residence. I have vision, where I was aimless, blind, and unraveled. I have been rescued like never before, because I required that kind of *love* intervention in the first place. It is as real as the words on this page. It started with a simple conversation with God, asking that He would not allow Malak's life to be wasted or our pain futile; asking for a visionary, spine-tingling opportunity to rise out of our ashes. Because God's promises are open to all of us.

Here is my remedy for your situation, regardless of the challenge:

Pray. I was raised with prayer. It alters us, though not always the situation. I have stained the floor of heaven with my prayers and seen the back alley of hell. I made many mistakes on the road to perdition and left a wake of pain for Chad and Grace. If a decade of obliteration is my battleground for a chance to be an uncommon woman of faith through adversity, I want God's quiet grace for that.

Believe. How do you find purpose for your life? It's your chance to make someone's life better. Because it's a privilege to do it. What makes you angry enough to be moved to action? The enormity of your conflict directly corresponds to the magnitude of your purpose. It's a sure sign your success is over that mountain. Because you are *that* powerful in Christ.

Say it over your life. Speak the blessings over your life. "I'm an author, speaker, world traveler, and a powerhouse woman of God. Everything I touch prospers, according to the Word of God. He commands blessings into my hands. His promises are yes and amen. I am forgiven. I am loved. I am beautiful." Who you see yourself as matters.

Write your creed. Outline your core life beliefs and guidelines. Write the dream/vision down.

Be thankful. List your bliss. Make a dream board. Make a point to take action, and send a thank-you card. Text a friend about how fantastic he or she is.

Listen to what inspires you on a regular basis. I walk every Saturday and listen to at least two sermons by those people who build up the promises of God inside me. They affect my mind-set and set the course for my day. Participating in a small-group Bible study on a weekly basis inspires my life too. I listen to music that is happy and inspires a heart of worship.

Someone prays for you by faith. God, interrupted and running into *your* midst for your sake, not His, I realize. His compass and direction leads us. I discovered that I am uniquely trained by my bruised heart for wreckage-mending, grief-championing, and as a gift to help others in this strange but exciting journey. He answers when you call Him. You never know what miracles are stitched into the lives of others or what they may yield in both of your lives. You can only step from where you stand. Take the risk. Believe. The God of the universe does indeed call you by name. He counts your tears according to His promises. He rebuilds your dreams better than you could ever do.

I can celebrate with hopeful anticipation what grand events and surprises lie ahead. I can't wait. I am celebrating health. Breath. Children. Friends to trust my scars and laughter with. A perfect sky. The vibrant color of Zetias in the park. Seasoned steak and carbohydrates. Movies and beaches. I am celebrating even heartache, because it will usher something wonderful and new if I let it in and hold fast to my golden thread on a stormy day.

The Golden Thread ... Life is remarkable. Etched are the high points and the low points, but in between is that small, loose thread on your lapel collar at the funeral. Your grandmother's pearls on your wedding day. The frayed edge on the empty pillowcase next to you. The penny on your office chair. The echoes of your children's words that speak to your jagged soul. The whisper in your ear that leads you onward. The Scripture scribbled on torn paper at the bottom of your pocket. A stranger's prayer. Your daddy's advice. Your mom's fingers through your hair. Your baby's head on your chest. But always, your heavenly Father's hand on your shoulder and His breath on your neck. The golden thread. You have one. I hope that you are aware of it now. More sure of your significance. More sure of your talents. Able to stand in a storm with more confidence but most assuredly, kneel with more certainty, that He is with you every second. Be sure. There will be storms. Unanswered questions. Empty hours. But God is far more real than we perceive. Resident in the space next to us in the seconds that pass. Immeasurable power. Unquenchable love. Ceaseless mercy. Ferocious warrior on our behalf.

When we say the name Jesus, there is power in the name. I like to contemplate what the power of His name must command. Does it beckon the earth to shift somewhere? Or cause a flock of birds to sing? Or heal a child in Nigeria, or whisper peace to a widow in China? Dispatch a miracle? Avert a crime? Cause the first kiss to destiny?

Go find that ridiculous, audacious, outrageous faith, and run with purpose.

"No eye has seen, nor ear has heard, nor mind conceived of what God has planned for those who love Him and are called according to His purpose." —1 Corinthians 2:9

ABOUT THE AUTHOR

K. Cates is an award-winning singer/songwriter who earned a Bachelor of Arts in Communications. She is on a lifelong pursuit to inspire others through faith and provoke purpose through adversity. Cates resides in Los Angeles where she working is on a second comedic novel, with her daughter.

Made in the USA
Middletown, DE
29 May 2016